lonely planet
Kids

THIS IS MY
WORLD

MEET 84 KIDS FROM
AROUND THE GLOBE

ACKNOWLEDGEMENTS

Publishing Director	Piers Pickard
Publisher	Hanna Otero
Project Editor	Mary Jones
Commissioning Editor	Christina Webb
Designer	Tina García
Art Director	Andy Mansfield
Print Production	Lisa Ford

Published in September 2019 by Lonely Planet Global Limited
CRN: 554153
ISBN: 978 1 78701 294 3
www.lonelyplanetkids.com
© Lonely Planet 2019

10 9 8 7 6 5 4 3 2 1

Printed in Malaysia

THANK YOU TO

Hannah Adisu, Kate Baker, Greg Bloom, Anthony Amos, Luan Angel, Sarah Anthony, Dora Ball, Raymond Bartlett, Robin Barton, Caroline Bell, Liam Bell, Julia Bergan, Joe Bindloss, Greg Bloom, Celeste Brash, Cathy Brown, Daisy Burt, Hannah Cartmel, Symon Chibaka, Serena Clark, Neill Coen, Katie Coffee, Sue Coffin, Lucy Corne, Laura Crawford, Joe Davis, Jacqui de Klerk, Violet Diallo, Anna Dvořákova, Alex Egerton, Helen Elfer, David Else, Ksenia Elzes, Seongae Eo, Trish Erber, Jen Feroze, Karen Finlay, Sunny Fitzgerald, Mary Fitzpatrick, Bailey Freeman, Ashley Garver, Duncan Garwood, Sopho Ghoghoberidze, David Gorvett, Will Gourlay, Gemma Graham, Njeri Gichuhi, Imogen Hall, Sandy Han, Laura Hamilton, Phil Harper, Mary Beth Willis Hedberg, Katie Holder, Amy Hornsby, Alexander Howard, Kathy Ishizuka, Jennifer Jammers, Teo Jioshvili, Alicia Johnson, Anna Kaminski, Barbara Noe Kennedy, Joanna Korbutiak, Jan Krieger, Stephen Lioy, Lydia Lloyd-Rose, Clementine Logan, Alex MacLeish, Flora Macqueen, Emily McAuliffe, Jacqueline McCann, Bruce McDonald, Maria McKenzie, Craig McLachlan, Clare Mercer, MaSovaida Morgan, Lucrezia Mutti, Mike Nelson, Sebastian Neylan, John Noble, Isabella Noble, Etain O'Carroll, Valentina Orsi, Theo Palaiopoulos, Nevena Paunovic, Katelyn Pennington, Claudia Peruccio, Matt Phillips, Ira Polianina, Tanny Por, Brandon Presser, Jacinda Quinn, Kevin Raub, Joe Revill, Claire Richardson, Jessica Ridgewell, Doug Rimington, Agnes Rivera, Flora Robertson, Kathryn Robinson, Lucinda Rouse, Loh Shee Keong, Tamara Sheward, Ileana Silvestre, James Smart, Emma Sparks, Tom Stainer, Sarah Stocking, Kate Sullivan, Andy Symington, Hélène Tassain-Perie, Stephanie Taylor, Pedro Teixeira, Marissa Tejada, Ryan Thomann, Titikorn Theerapatvong, Kira Tverskaya, Anna Tyler, Giuliana Valle, Angel Vañó, Brana Vladisavljevic, Mara Vorhees, Tasmin Waby, Jenny Walker, Clifton Wilkinson, Allyson Wiley, Asnakech Wujira, Guan Yuanyuan, Chris Zeiher.

FOREWORD

If you were asked to tell someone on the other side of the world about yourself, where would you start?

Perhaps you'd tell us a little bit about your favourite hobbies, the games or pranks you play on your family or what you want to be when you grow up. Would you include a selfie and a family photo? A cute snap of your puppy or that cool shot of you playing your favourite sport? What if you had to paint a picture of your home, school or town for someone who had never been there?

Sharing Their World

The 84 children you're about to meet share what's unique about their lives – local foods and popular sports, unusual weather and landscapes, different types of families – but they also show us how much children have in common no matter where they live. You may be surprised to discover how many interests you share with a child who lives thousands of miles away! To create this book, we reached out to cattle ranchers in the Australian outback, inhabitants of a fishing capital in Greenland, city dwellers living among skyscrapers in Nigeria and many more families! By turning to Lonely Planet's global community, we connected with dozens of families. As a result, this book represents life on six continents in more than 70 countries.

Helping Children Facing Conflict

Sadly, not every child grows up in a peaceful place. Lonely Planet Kids partnered with the nonprofit organisation War Child UK to share the lives of children who have grown up in areas of armed conflict. War Child supports children who live in places torn apart by war and helps provide them with the chance of a better future. Among other children in this book who live in difficult circumstances, you will meet Esther, who lives in Uganda, and Yousef, who lives in a refugee camp in Jordan. A portion of the money raised by the sale of *This Is My World* will go to War Child UK and their efforts to help Esther, Yousef and other children from war-torn areas.

HOW TO USE THIS BOOK

Work your way from A to Z to meet the children of *This Is My World*.

Map

Looking for something specific? The key at the bottom of the map on pages 6–7 shows the name of every child featured in this book. Find the numbered dot on the map to see where the child lives, then go to the page number shown inside the dot to read about her or him.

Flags

The flag of the nation or territory in which each child lives appears in the upper left corner of every entry.

Globes

A globe in the upper left corner of each spread illustrates where to find the country featured on the pages. Globes are colour coded by continent: African countries are shown on orange globes, Asian on dark purple, European on blue, North American on green, Oceanian on yellow, and South American on light purple.

Fast Facts

Fast Fact boxes appear throughout the book and present fun information or explain words, places or concepts that may be unfamiliar.

My Three Words

In addition to telling us about their homes, hobbies and families, some of the kids in this book gave us three adjectives to describe themselves. What three words would you use to tell about yourself?

HOLA

こんにちは

Hello

Salut

здравствуй

WHERE WE LIVE...

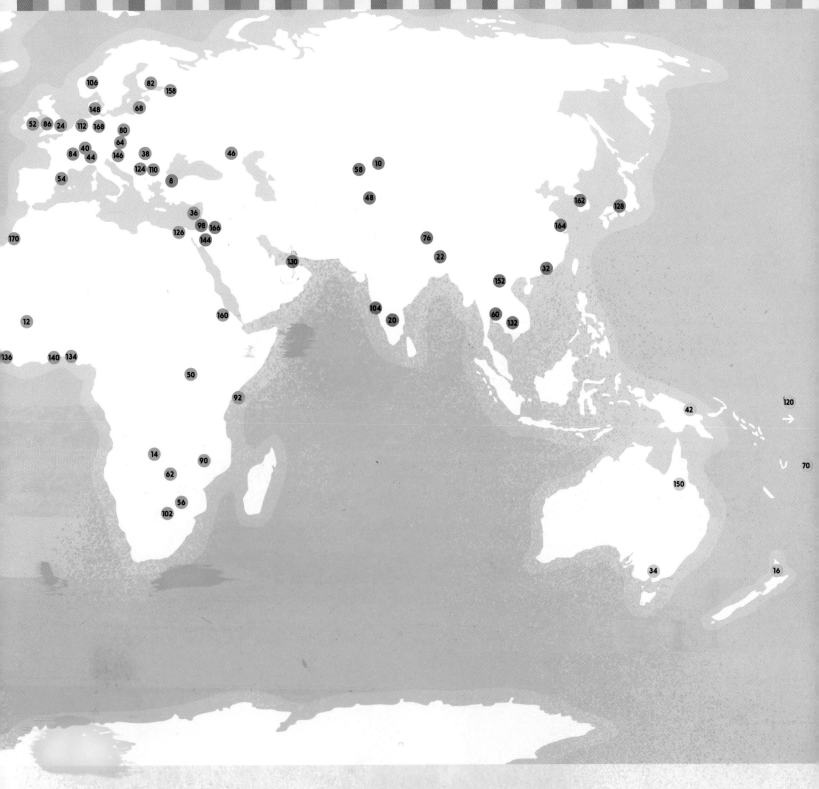

138 Iceland — Raphaël
52 Ireland — Ethan
44 Italy — Elia
124 Kosovo — Nea
68 Lithuania — Ilja
106 Norway — Mari
46 Russia — Elsyata
158 Russia — Victor
38 Serbia — Djurdja
146 Slovenia — Stela
54 Spain — Gaia
40 Switzerland — Dylan
86 Wales, UK — Kelsie

North America

18 Barbados — Arjun
74 Canada — Jaylynn
100 Costa Rica — Lluvia
28 Greenland — Aviana
72 Guatemala — Javier
88 Jamaica — Kitara
156 Mexico — Valentina
78 Trinidad and Tobago — Jordan
26 USA — Audrey
96 USA — Leo
114 USA — Maximus
122 USA — Nathen

Oceania

120 American Samoa — Michael
34 Australia — Cooper
150 Australia — Temperance
70 Fiji — Jack
16 New Zealand — Anneke
42 Papua New Guinea — Elaine

South America

154 Argentina — Tobias
108 Brazil — Marina
94 Chile — Laura
116 Colombia — Mayra
118 Ecuador — Melani
66 Guyana — Ikie
142 Paraguay — Shawn

Turkey

ADA
Age 7

My name is Ada, and I live in Istanbul, Turkey.

ISTANBUL

Istanbul is very crowded. There are many buildings and skyscrapers around. My favourite place to visit in Istanbul is the Basilica Cistern, which lies beneath the city. It was built in the sixth century and provided a water filtration system for the Great Palace of Constantinople and Topkapı Palace.

MY THREE WORDS
Excited, Funny, Smart

MY HOMES
I live in a flat with my mother and grandmother close to the Bosphorus Strait. I go to my father's for the weekends. He lives in a different flat. I also have my grandfather's house and farm in a village.
I go there in the summertime.

MY FAMILY
My mother is a teacher, and my father is a tour guide. I do not have any brothers or sisters.

Basilica Cistern

PURR-FECT PET

I have a little cat. Her name is Deniz.

FEELING SPORTY

I like to play volleyball. There is a team at my school, and I want to be part of it. I also like to play table tennis at school.

I am learning to play guitar.

MY SCHOOL

My school is not very far from our flat. It has an art gallery, a big library and a sports centre. There are 23 students in my class. I like creative drama, ballet, chess and visual arts. My least favourite subject is Turkish.

YUM!

My favourite food is homemade meatballs and chips. My grandmother is an expert at it.

Kazakhstan

AGATHA
AGE 7

My name is Agatha. I live in Almaty, Kazakhstan.

ALMATY

I love Almaty. There are some toy shops and entertaining places such as a trampoline centre. I love the mountains with their berries in the summer and skiing in the winter. There's a university located close to our home, so there are lots of students on the streets.

MY FAMILY

My mother, father, my lovely cat, Kitty, and I are in my family. My family is small but it is very united. We like to go to the mountains in the summer and the skating rink in the winter. My mother works for a bank, and my father is a travel manager.

MY THREE WORDS

CHEERFUL

PRETTY

GIRL

Skiing, ice skating, cycling and boxing are popular in Kazakhstan.

MY SCHOOL

I love my school very much. It is not far from my home. My class consists of 40 children. My favourite school subject is art because we paint a lot and do some crafts.

GOT TALENT?

My favourite holiday is my birthday because of the warm wishes, fun and gifts. I celebrate my birthday with my parents and friends, and we put on a talent show that is simply fantastic. Every child or group chooses a role, and then we show off our talents. It can be dancing or singing songs.

HOME SWEET HOME

We live in a flat, and I really like my home.

I like practising karate.

IN BLOOM

We have lots of different kinds of weather in our city — a hot summer, cold winter, rainy autumn and a warm spring full of flowers.

Mali

AMINATA
AGE 9

My name is Aminata.
I live in Bamako, Mali.

MALI

Mali is in West Africa, and there are lots and lots of languages here. Lots of people understand Bambara, and some people also learn to speak French, but English isn't spoken much.

MY THREE WORDS
Intelligent, Dancer, Kangaba*

*a historic town in Mali where my grandmother grew up

MY FAMILY

My family is very big. I live with my aunt and uncle, and I am the youngest of six children. I fight with my siblings a lot, but we also get along well together.

If I were an animal, I would be an elephant because they like to make lots of noise!

Niger River

MY HOME

I live in Bamako. We live in a house where over 30 people sleep. My aunt and uncle rent two rooms for our family, and my aunt also has a big kitchen outside. We spend most of our time outside where it is cooler and we eat and prepare food.

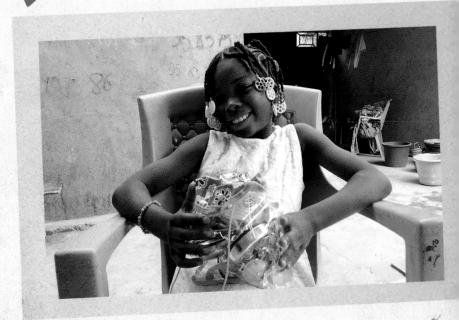

DUSTY LAND

We are close to the Sahara, so it is very dry and dusty here. We don't have the sea because Mali is surrounded by other countries, but there is the Niger River which is about a ten-minute walk from my house.

LET'S COOK!

I love cooking because we cook for everybody, and then everybody is full. I prepare food with my Aunt Hawa, my sisters and Sacko, who works and lives with us. We prepare a different sauce each day to go with rice. My favourite is *yassa*. It's made with onions, carrots and beef.

BABYSITTER

I love babies and looking after them. I also really like to work on the computer, but my school doesn't have any. I love dancing and singing, too.

MUSIC ALL AROUND

My family are known as *griots*, and they play music for a living. Aunt Hawa is a singer and performs all the time at weddings and baptisms, and she often goes to Europe and America with her group, Trio Da Kali. Uncle Demba plays the guitar and an instrument called the *ngoni*.

My aunt and her group, Trio Da Kali

Fast Fact: In ancient Africa, *griots* served as the musicians, storytellers and historians of their villages. Today, the griot tradition continues in parts of West Africa. Modern griots are often travelling musicians.

Zambia

ANNA & GIVEN

Anna and Given are two of more than 30 orphans who live in an orphanage in Zambezi, Zambia.

Ages 9 & 11

Fast Fact:
Zambezi is a town in northwestern Zambia. The Zambezi River – the fourth largest river in Africa – flows nearby. Hippopotamuses and crocodiles can be found in its waters.

OUR FAMILY
We live in an orphanage. We have 16 'sisters' and 15 'brothers' here. The oldest is sister Edina. The youngest is brother Michek. Everyone helps each other – doing the washing and studying.

OUR HOME
We sleep in dorms. We are grouped together – boys in one dorm, girls in the other. We eat together in the dining room.

FAVOURITE SUBJECT

My favourite subject is English, and my least favourite subject is maths. I want to be a doctor and heal people.

My favourite subject is maths. My least favourite subject is Lunda (a Burundi language). I want to be a pilot.

FUN AND GAMES

I like to play baseball.

I like to play chess.

FAVOURITE FOODS

My favourite meal is meat and *nshima* (a thick porridge made with cornmeal).

My favourite meal is rice and beans.

EEK!

I am scared of snakes. There are big snakes here.

I am scared of frogs. I don't know why!

Study time

Fun time

New Zealand

ANNEKE
AGE 12

My name is Anneke. I live
in Auckland, New Zealand.

MY THREE WORDS
Kind, Creative, Clever

AUCKLAND
Nicknamed the 'City of Sails',
Auckland is known for its many
sailing boats and yachts. It is
surrounded by beaches. Some are
great for surfing. The Sky Tower
is a well-known landmark. It has a
rotating restaurant and its
own vertical
bungee jump.

Where I live on the North Shore,
we are surrounded by a lot of
beautiful beaches.

MY FAMILY
I have a huge extended family on my Samoan/
Tokelauan side (mum's), but my Japanese/
British side (dad's) is a lot smaller. I live with
my parents and my brother, who is five years
older than me.

Sky Tower

Auckland

CLOUDS AND KIWIS

The Māori name for New Zealand is Aotearoa. It means 'Land of the Long White Cloud'. Aotearoa is a very multicultural place. A lot of the people who are born and raised in Aotearoa call themselves 'Kiwis'.

Fast Fact: Māori are the indigenous — or native — people of New Zealand.

NATIONAL PASTIME

The most popular sport that New Zealanders watch and support is rugby. The only sport that I play is netball. Netball season is in the winter, so sometimes we have to play in the pouring rain!

TOO CUTE

I don't have a favourite animal, but I loved playing with the neighbour's cats when I was little, and I like being around them. I love anything playful and cuddly!

UPHILL CLIMB

It is very green and hilly where I live. My bedroom window is blocked by tall trees, and I have to walk up a hill to get to school, so I get a good workout!

FAVOURITE SUBJECTS

At school, I like programming because I can create cool things, and I like cooking because I love seeing how the final product will turn out!

Barbados

ARJUN
Age 7

My name is Arjun. I live in Bridgetown, Barbados.

Meal time

MY THREE WORDS
Absolutely Animal Crazy

BARBADOS

Barbados is flat and rocky. You are never very far away from the beach since the island is so small. The weather is usually sunny and perfect for going outside to play.

MY FAMILY

I live with my mum, Chrystabel, and my sister, Katherine, in a house in the city. My sister and I share a bedroom, and we have a small back garden. We love to play outside because it is much cooler than inside. My dad, Jason, lives in St. Lucia, another island in the Caribbean.

SAY CHEESE!
I love taking photos of my family and animals.

FEEL THE BEAT
I enjoy practising my guitar. Drumming is fun, too.

WARM WELCOME
The people of Barbados are very friendly and patriotic. When my family moved here from St. Lucia, I was scared that I would not make friends. Now I have lots of friends at school and in my community.

I LOVE TO LEARN ABOUT LIVING THINGS.

Turtle discovery

MY SCHOOL
I go to a special school for children with autism (like me) and other special needs. I love helping the children in wheelchairs around the playground. I like science and geography, and I love talking about all the different animals you can find on each continent.

BEACH LOVER
I like the beach the most. The water is warm and clear and never too far away.

India

ARJUN
Age 8

My name is Arjun, and I live in Bengaluru (Bangalore), India.

MY THREE WORDS

Honest
Kind
Talkative

BENGALURU

I live in southern India, but I belong to the Bengali community. We love our art, poetry and culture. Bengali food is famous, as are Bengali writers.

MY FAMILY

In Bengaluru, my family includes my father, mother, my four-year-old brother, Agni, and me. In Kolkata — where my parents come from — I have many grandparents, uncles, aunts and cousins. My grandparents come to live with us for many months so then we have a bigger family.

Bengaluru

BASKETBALL

I play basketball every Saturday and Sunday morning with my friends.

RAILWAY FAN

I love trains more than anything else. I know all the types of railway engines that run in India, their make, their history and everything about them. I want to work on researching railways and railway engines when I grow up.

FIRST SNOW

Bengaluru is pleasantly warm, even in the winter. I love the snow, though. This year, I went to the Himalayan state of Sikkim to see snow for the first time in my life.

C-H-A-M-P

I am a spelling bee champion. I recently qualified for the state level competition and have applied for the nationals.

FAVOURITE FOODS

I absolutely love to eat. My mum makes *luchi* (fried bread) and potato curry as a special breakfast, and that is my favourite food in the world. I also love biryani (a spicy rice dish with meat, fish or vegetables). I can eat biryani all day.

MY HOME

I live in a seventh-floor flat, and I love looking out from the balcony because I can see treetops with birds in them.

21

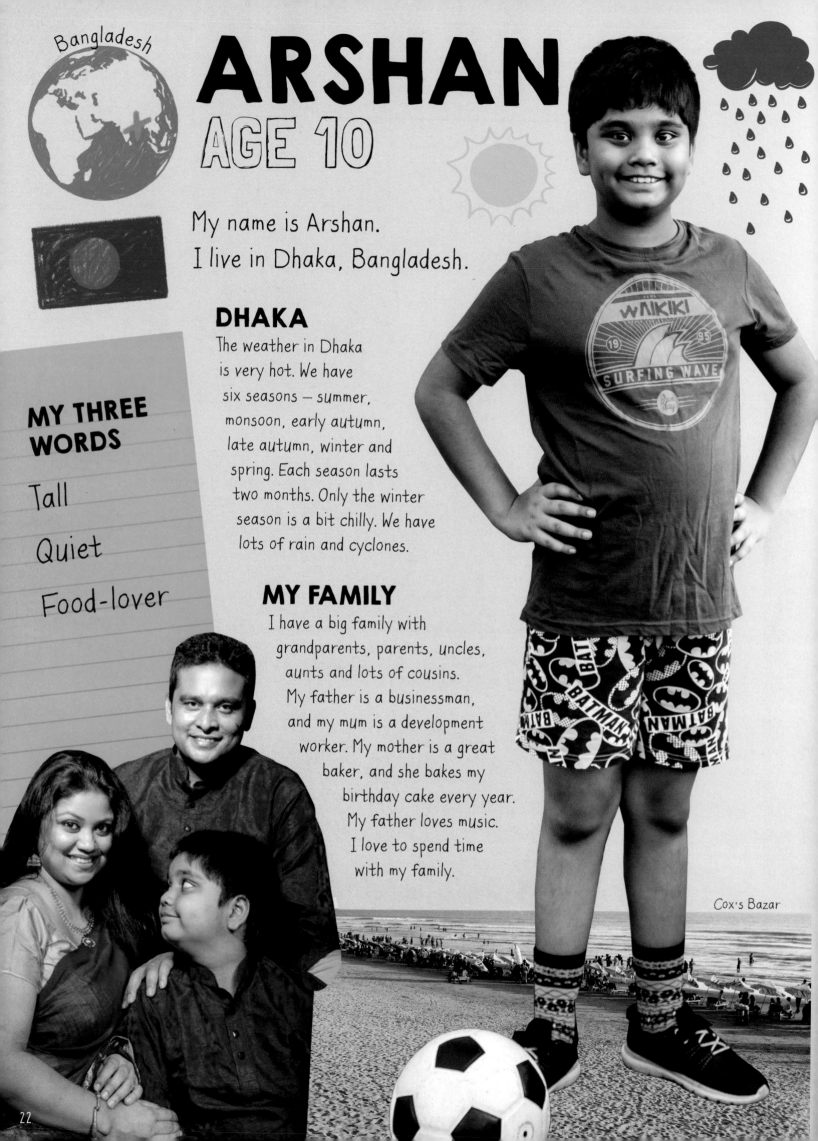

Bangladesh

ARSHAN
AGE 10

My name is Arshan.
I live in Dhaka, Bangladesh.

DHAKA

The weather in Dhaka is very hot. We have six seasons — summer, monsoon, early autumn, late autumn, winter and spring. Each season lasts two months. Only the winter season is a bit chilly. We have lots of rain and cyclones.

MY FAMILY

I have a big family with grandparents, parents, uncles, aunts and lots of cousins. My father is a businessman, and my mum is a development worker. My mother is a great baker, and she bakes my birthday cake every year. My father loves music. I love to spend time with my family.

MY THREE WORDS

Tall

Quiet

Food-lover

Cox's Bazar

22

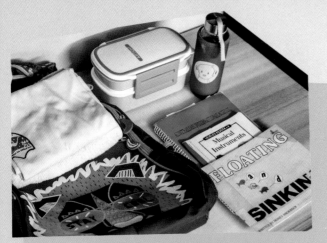

MY BACKPACK

DID IT MYSELF

I make DIY things. I made a Peter Pan wall in my bedroom with my mum's help, and a traffic signal light from my make-and-do activity book.

MY BREAKFAST

CAPITAL LIFE

I live in a busy capital. My home is beside a big beautiful lake called Hatirjheel. There are lots of markets and tall buildings around, but my home has green fields and lots of trees.

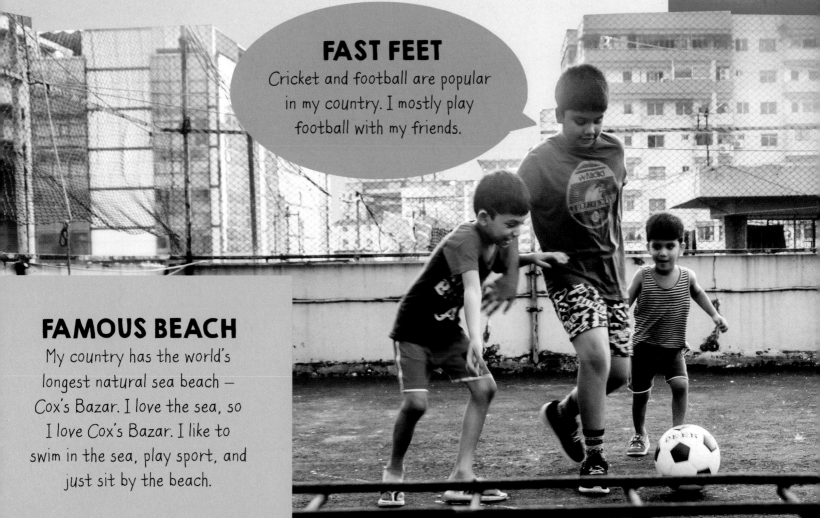

FAST FEET
Cricket and football are popular in my country. I mostly play football with my friends.

FAMOUS BEACH

My country has the world's longest natural sea beach — Cox's Bazar. I love the sea, so I love Cox's Bazar. I like to swim in the sea, play sport, and just sit by the beach.

England

ATIYA
AGE 11

My name is Atiya. I live in the Elephant and Castle section of London, England, in the United Kingdom.

MY THREE WORDS

Mature
Artistic
Determined

LONDON

I live in a bustling city where I am surrounded by skyscrapers. The shops are a short walk away from my home, and there is a buzz of friendliness. My community — Elephant and Castle — is known for its spirit. The people are vibrant and quirky and representative of true London.

MY FAMILY

I live with my mum and dad. I have a huge extended family and lots of amazing cousins. I am an only child, but I am surrounded by friends who are like sisters. Together we watch TV, go exploring and sightsee famous landmarks around London.

Fast Fact: England, Wales, Scotland and Northern Ireland make up the United Kingdom. England is the largest of the four countries.

EXPRESS YOURSELF

Dancing makes me feel alive. I want to be a street dancer and perform dances from my heritage – Singaporean and Jamaican. As a mixed-race female, I want to inspire people to do what they love without limits and be proud of who they are.

MEET PUPPY-CAT

I have a pet cat named Lily. She's a little gem. Unlike most cats, she loves cuddling up. She almost thinks she's a puppy!

SWEET SUMMER

Summer is my favourite. The summers in London are hot and sticky, but the open spaces of the parks are a great place to unwind with a picnic and an ice cream.

THE WRITE STUFF

I am very creative and an aspiring author. I write my own stories and hope to have them published one day.

SEASIDE ADVENTURE

My friends and I went to Brighton Beach for a school trip. Some of us had never been to the seaside before. It was unfortunately a pebbly beach, but the waves were amazing.

MY HOME

I live in a flat with two bedrooms. I have the most spectacular view of The Shard from my balcony.

The Shard

AUDREY
Age 10

My name is Audrey.
I live in Oak Park,
Illinois, USA.

MY THREE WORDS
Fun, Cool, Creative

On a climbing wall

OAK PARK

In the Midwestern United States, it is very, very flat. We live 11 km (7 miles) east of Chicago, and it is so flat that you can see the skyscrapers downtown from where we live. Chicago is on Lake Michigan, which is so large it looks like an ocean.

MY FAMILY

We are a family of four. There is me, my older brother, Alistair, my mum, Vanessa, and my dad, Michael. My brother and I fight lit-er-ally all the time, but he is funny sometimes. My mum and dad both work in downtown Chicago. My dad is also a musician who plays the drums.

Chicago

My room

MY HOUSE

Our house is two storeys plus a basement and an attic, and it was built 100 years ago. When I grow up, I hope I am like my mum . . . but maybe with a messier house. My room is the only room with any clutter in the whole house!

SUMMER FUN

Summer is really fun because there is a public pool close to my house with lots of kids to hang out with. It can get hot and humid in the summer, so the pool's a must.

DREAMING BIG

When I grow up, I'd like to be an artist, a YouTuber or an actress. I would maybe be in a band, too. I don't take piano lessons, but we have a piano and drums, and I like playing musical instruments. I like discovering new music.

Making music with Dad

SPORTS FANS

In Chicago, people LOVE baseball. It is a sports city. My dad loves the Chicago White Sox baseball team and the Chicago Bears football team. I like gymnastics, dance and ice skating.

MY FAVOURITE ANIMAL

If I had to pick my favourite animal, I would say dogs because we have two mini goldendoodles, and they are the cutest doggies ever. But, I like all animals!

FEEL THE CHILL

Sometimes it gets so cold that school is cancelled. They don't cancel school for snow, but they cancel school when the wind chill is -29°C (-20°F) or below.

Greenland

AVIANA
Age 9

MY THREE WORDS

Creative

Caring

Glad

My name is Aviana. I live in Nuuk, Greenland.

NUUK

Nuuk is a small capital with 18,000 people. In the winter, it is cold with a lot of snow. Sometimes we have very big storms. In the summer, it is nice and sunny.

MY FAMILY

I live with my parents and my older brother, Nicolay, who is 17 years old. I also have two grown-up sisters — Maria and Louise — and a grown-up brother named Michael.
My mother, Tina, works in a ministry, and my dad, Sakarias, works for the parliament.

OUR HOUSE

We live in a house by a big fjord with a lot of whales and seabirds. Sometimes we can hear the whales. We have a small garden with a lot of purple flowers in summer.

Fast Fact: A fjord is a long, narrow body of water with steep cliffs or rocky slopes on either side.

FAST BOATS

If we want to go to another town, we have to go by plane or by boat. The next town is Maniitsoq — half an hour away by plane and four hours away by a fast boat.

We can go on boat trips in the summer and ski in the winter.

I LIKE LIVING IN NUUK A LOT.

← My dad with a snow crab

WILD LIFE

In Nuuk, people like to go hiking, fishing and hunting.

LIGHT SHOW

In the winter, there are a lot of northern lights, and in the summer, the sun shines all night.

I like to make creative things with my hands.

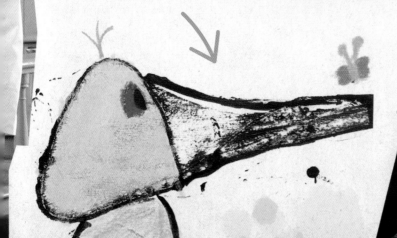

Senegal

BAYE MAKHTAR
Age 8

My name is Baye Makhtar.
I live in Saint-Louis, Senegal.

SAINT-LOUIS

My hometown, Saint-Louis, is located at the mouth of the Senegal River, where it meets the sea. The oldest part of the town is on an island in the river with a long bridge connecting it to the mainland. I live on the mainland.

MY FAMILY

I have an older sister and an older brother, and I live with several other children — Thiané (age 17), Ndella (age 14) and Ndeye Mareme (age 13) — so our family is quite big. My mother works at home.

Me and Ndella

FAVOURITE FOOD

My favourite food is *yassa*. It's chicken with rice and an onion sauce. It's one of the most popular dishes in Senegal.

Pirogues

STREET FOOTALL

I love playing football in the street every evening with my friends. I also love the board game Ludo™ which I play with the other children in my family.

COOL TRIP

I'd like to visit France because I've never been, and I'd like to see snow.

GONE FISHING

Saint-Louis is known for its large fishing community and the fishermen's brightly painted wooden boats called pirogues.

Saint-Louis

MY SCHOOL

I go to a primary school in Saint-Louis. It is one of the best. There are hundreds of children in my school and 58 in my class. I can walk there from home in five minutes. My favourite subject is maths because it's easy.

MY HOUSE

I live in a big house with three floors. There's a roof terrace on top and a courtyard when you enter through the front door. There is also a papaya tree in the back garden, which produces fruit during the rainy season.

31

Hong Kong

BRENO
Age 9

My name is Breno.
I live in Ma Wan,
Hong Kong.

Fast Fact:
A former British colony, Hong Kong became a special administrative region (SAR) of China in 1997.

MA WAN

I live on a small island in Hong Kong called Ma Wan. It's pretty hot. It does not snow here even during winter. There are typhoons in summer.

MY THREE WORDS

Average, Jolly, Fat

MY FAMILY

I have my mum, dad and a brother who is five years younger than me. My dad goes to work a lot — even on Saturdays and Sundays. My mum and a domestic helper cook, clean and take care of us at home.

Fast Fact: Dim sum is a Chinese cuisine made up of small dishes, such as dumplings, that are usually steamed or fried and often served in steamer baskets.

DIM SUM
My mum likes to take me and my cousin Hero to eat Chinese dim sum with my grandpa on Sundays.

Hong Kong has a lot of tall skyscrapers. There are a lot of mountains, too.

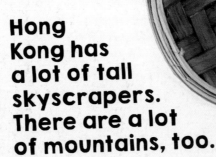

DREAM JOBS
When I grow up, I want to be a video game designer or take on my uncle's job and forge metals into railings.

GOOD FORTUNE
During Chinese New Year, we decorate our block of flats in red and give out red packets – little red envelopes with money inside – to whoever comes over to celebrate. All my uncles and aunties give me red envelopes, too. I have a lot of money on that day!

NO CARS
There are only about 30 buildings in our Ma Wan community, so not too many people live here. Because Ma Wan is environmentally friendly, no private cars can drive in. We have a shuttle bus that takes us to the city.

SCHOOL DAYS
My favourite subject is science because it is interesting and fun, and my least favourite is Mandarin. The teachers in the schools give children too much homework. Kids in Hong Kong get a lot of tutoring after school.

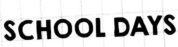

Chinese New Year snacks and red envelopes

View from Ma Wan

COOPER
Age 12

My name is Cooper. I live in Melbourne, Victoria, Australia.

MY THREE WORDS

Adventurous
Interesting
Loving

MELBOURNE

We live in a suburb of Melbourne and can walk or wheel to the beach from our house in ten minutes. I love being outdoors and exploring.

MY FAMILY

My family has five people in it. I am the eldest child, and my siblings are nine and six years old. My sister loves to draw and read, and my brother loves Lego™ and riding his scooter. I like cooking and playing with my Nerf™ guns.

NO WALLS

I don't really enjoy the repetitive nature of classes. I like world schooling better!

WORLD TRAVELLER

My family like to travel together! I have been to 24 countries so far. I loved seeing pandas in Chengdu, China.

I love surfing each summer!

MY HOBBIES

I love reading and researching about World War II and all history. I also love cars and shoes!

Melbourne

OLD FRIENDS

Most of my friends are older than me because I like to talk to adults and learn new things. I have always been around adults as I couldn't move like other kids when I was smaller.

AROUND TOWN

We can be in the city of Melbourne in one hour. I love exploring the city and checking out the amazing street art and food.

MY HOUSE

My house is very special to me because I can be independent here. It is specially made to be all flat for my wheelchair. It has large wide doors and a bathroom that has no barriers. I also have a therapy pool and a gym.

Cyprus

DANIEL
Age 11

My name is Daniel.
I live in Alsancak,
Cyprus.

MY THREE WORDS
CREATIVE, SOCIAL, CALM

ALSANCAK

We live on an island called Cyprus with a big sea called the Mediterranean Sea. Cyprus is split into two parts: Greek and Turkish. I would say that on the Greek side, the population is bigger since there are more cities than towns. The Turkish side is less developed and life here is quieter.

MY FAMILY

My dad, mum and brother are in my family. My brother is almost six years old, and he likes to play chess a LOT. We all have mixed nationalities. My dad is half Italian and half Turkish, my mum is completely Polish and my brother and I were born in Italy, but we've lived in different countries.

COLLECTING OLIVES

Cyprus is known for fresh vegetables and fruits — especially olives.

MY FAVOURITE ANIMAL

Cats! My cat is a Russian blue. We also have over seven stray cats come to our house every day for food.

IN THE GARDEN

Our home is a regular house with a garden and a pool. Our island is boiling hot, and it only rains between December and March. During the summer, we jump in the pool every day. My dad takes good care of the pool, and my mum takes care of the garden. I help them sometimes.

TURTLE ISLAND

Cyprus protects sea turtles from danger.

SNOW FUN

On the southern side of Cyprus, there are bigger mountains called Troodos. There it snows a lot in the winter, and we even ski there.

SET SAIL

My favourite sport is sailing. I mostly go out with my friends since many of the boats need two people. It sounds pretty hard to sail, but it only takes about four lessons to sail the sea alone or with friends.

Serbia

DJURDJA
AGE 9

My name is Djurdja. I live in Belgrade, Serbia.

BELGRADE

There are lots of people in Belgrade, and it's crowded, especially in the city centre. There are lots of schools and nursery schools, shops and cars.

MY FAMILY

In my family, there is my mum, my dad, my younger sister, Iskra, and me. I love my parents because they are good: they take us to museums, and they both make good lunches. Sometimes my dad starts a food fight at dinner, and Mum gets really angry at us if food hits the wall!

MY THREE WORDS

SUPER

COOL

CRAZY

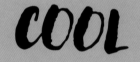

Belgrade

JUMP TO IT

I like to play elastics. Two girls (or chairs) hold the elastic rope. My sister and I play a game where you need to step over the rope in an exact order. If you do it right, you set the rope higher and try again!

MY LUNCH

Lunch is the main meal in Serbia. We have soup, salad, sausage pastry and lentils made by Mum. Mum also cooks vegetables, fried chicken, moussaka and goulash, and Dad usually makes pasta.

HOT AND COLD

The weather in Belgrade is moody. When it's cold in the morning, our mum puts tons of clothes on us. Then it gets warm later on, and it's hard to walk around with all these clothes on!

SWEET TWEET

I have a lovebird parrot named Kitya.

BEST ADVENTURE

My favourite place that I've visited is Kopaonik Mountain in Serbia. I was there in the summertime, and I loved it because there were many forests. We also rode in a cable car.

MY HOME

I live in a flat. It's nice. I love it. It has three rooms, and my sister and I have our own little rooms. The bathroom is also small, and I would like it to be bigger.

Switzerland

DYLAN
Age 10

My name is Dylan.
I live in Zug,
Switzerland.

MY THREE
WORDS

Funny

Clever

Ticklish

ZUG

Zug is known for its cherry season, its lake and its mountain — the Zugerberg. I don't really like to eat cherries, but people here do. In the summer, we like to swim in the lake. I like living in the middle of Switzerland because I can visit other countries easily.

MY FAMILY

There are three kids in my family as well as Mama and Papa. I have two sisters. I love that my older sister, Alexandra, plays Lego™ with me and helps me with my homework, and I love that my younger sister, Zoey, gives me lots of hugs.

INSTANT CLASSIC

I have played the violin for five years. My favourite song to play on it is 'Harry's Wondrous World' from the Harry Potter films.

WOODWORKER

I like to go hiking in the woods. I take my Swiss Army knife with me and create things out of wood.

Hallo Hi

MY BREAKFAST

MY HOME

We live in a flat. My grandparents live upstairs in another flat, and my uncle and aunt also live in the building. We live near the train station, which makes it easy to get to the next busy city or the airport.

FRIENDSHIP BUILDER

I have lots of different friends. Some speak German, others speak English. I like to play Lego™ with them, and the board game Machi Koro™.

AUSSIE FUN

My favourite place to visit is Australia. My mum was born there. I like to visit my family, see Australian animals and go to the beach.

41

Papua New Guinea

ELAINE
AGE 9

My name is Elaine.
I live in Kina Beach,
Madang, Papua New Guinea.

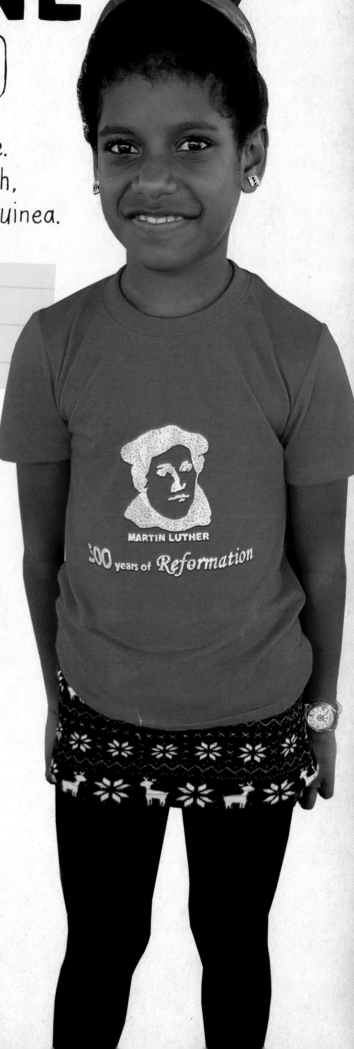

MY THREE WORDS
I Am Pretty!

KINA BEACH

We live in a rented house
by the sea, and our suburb
is called Kina Beach. It has
lots of flowers and trees
and is a peaceful and quiet
neighbourhood.

MY FAMILY

I have two brothers and
two older sisters. My dad is
an aircraft engineer while
my mum is a stay-at-home
parent. We are not allowed to
fight in our family.

There is a butterfly farm in our province.

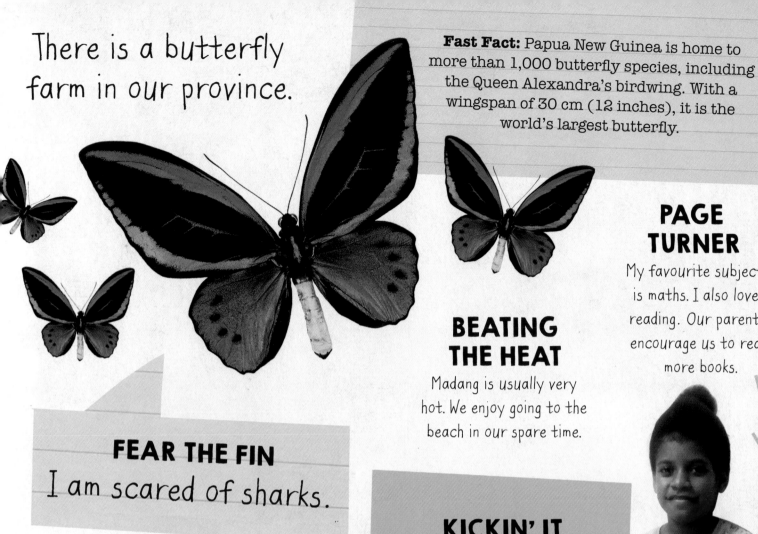

PAGE TURNER

My favourite subject is maths. I also love reading. Our parents encourage us to read more books.

BEATING THE HEAT

Madang is usually very hot. We enjoy going to the beach in our spare time.

FEAR THE FIN

I am scared of sharks.

KICKIN' IT

I love football, but I only play at home with my siblings and friends. Football is the most popular sport in my area.

CREATIVE COOK

I love cooking and baking different kinds of cakes. I want to be a chef.

43

Italy

ELIA
AGE 7

My name is Elia. I live in Turin, Italy.

TURIN

My family lives in a multicultural neighbourhood in the centre of Turin. It's between the train station and a big park called Parco del Valentino, which is crossed by the Po River.

MY THREE WORDS

KIND

DREAMER

SENSITIVE

FAMILY RESTAURANT

I'd like to be a chef like my grandmother. She runs the family restaurant with my grandfather in a small town on Lake Garda.

MY FAMILY

My family is medium-sized: me, my brother, Mum and Dad. My brother's name is Ettore. He is almost five, and he has red hair and freckles, while I'm blonde with no freckles.

TERRACE GARDEN

We live in a flat on the sixth floor of our building. There is a small veranda and a terrace where my dad grows plants and flowers.

MY FAVOURITE TOY

SKI TRAIN

Turin is located in the northwestern part of Italy, near the Alps and the French border. It's so near the Alps that during winter you can catch the train and go skiing.

AROUND TOWN

I like Rino from the newspaper shop. He's kind and always gives us some sweets. I also like the lady at the bakery. I often go there with my brother. She always gives us one *grissino* (breadstick) each.

MAKING A SPLASH

Summer is quite hot. When the city is really hot, my mum takes us to the fountains in front of the Royal Palace where there are always kids playing in the water. I like diving and swimming in the pool during the summer, too.

Russia

ELSYATA AGE 8

My name is Elsyata. I live in Elista, Kalmykia, Russia.

MY THREE WORDS

BEAUTIFUL

FUNNY   CLEVER

ELISTA

I live in a small village near a bigger city called Elista. In the spring, we have tulips blooming, and in the late summer there are lotus flowers. Summers are usually ve-e-ery hot, and winters have very little snow.

Wearing my national costume — a traditional Kalmykian girl's dress

MY FAMILY

My family is not too big — it's my mum, dad, brother and me. My younger brother is five years old. Papa works at the bank. Mama works as an accountant and likes to sew. Mostly she makes dresses for me.

WEEKEND STROLL

On weekends, people usually go walking around the pagoda, our Buddhist temple. People meet there and walk. It's like the main square of the town.

Golden Abode of Buddha Shakyamuni

Fast Fact: Kalmykia, Russia is the only area in Europe where Buddhism is the central religion.

CHESS CITY

There's a chess palace where people can come and play chess, and we have competitions as well.

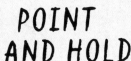

POINT AND HOLD

I dance and do gymnastics. Kalamykian wrestling is the most popular sport where I live. They do all kinds of holds, but I don't do it.

MY BREAKFAST

Scrambled eggs, *djomba* (Kalmykian tea with milk and salt) and *boortsog* (pieces of dough fried in butter with blackcurrant jam).

TULIP TIME

There's a tulip festival in the spring, around April. People go to the steppe (grassland) to see the tulips, which are usually red and yellow.

MY FAVORITE ANIMAL
Cats

Afghanistan

EMAN
Age 7

My name is Eman. I live in Taloqan in Takhar province, Afghanistan.

MY THREE WORDS
Stubborn, Adventurous, Persuasive

TALOQAN

This is a very traditional and conservative society. Takhar province is a green place, with a lot of trees, agricultural land and green hills. We live far from the city. It is calm and not crowded.

MY HOME

We live in a house. It is very small. We have only three rooms. One room is for guests because in Afghanistan, we host a lot of friends and relatives. One room is the dining room where the kids also sleep, and the other one is my parents' bedroom.

MY FAMILY

I have a big family: my father and mother and five kids — all of them boys! My oldest brother is 15 years old and the youngest is about two and a half years old. My mother works as the head of a regional management office, and my father is studying in India to earn a master's degree.

Eid cookies

TIME TO CELEBRATE!

My favourite holiday is Eid. This is a holiday in Muslim culture. Every year, there are two Eids in six days. In the first Eid — right after Ramadan — people buy new clothes, and I am very happy because I can see all my friends. I visit every friend at their house, and we all eat and drink.

MY FAVOURITE FOOD

My favourite food is *manto*. It's meat cooked with flour and eaten with something that is like yoghurt.

BIG GOALS

I would like to become the best surgeon in my country so my people wouldn't have to travel abroad for treatment. I also like games, and I would like to write games for kids.

CHANGING SEASONS

We have four seasons. Spring is very green, and summer is not very hot. A lot of fruits grow then. In autumn, there is no rain, and winter is cold with a lot of snow. I don't like the cold because we don't have proper heating.

TACKLING TAE KWON DO

I practise tae kwon do. It is one of the few organised sports in Takhar. I have been doing it for almost two years now.

My province, Takhar

Uganda

ESTHER
AGE 8

My name is Esther, and I live in northern Uganda.

UGANDA

Where I was born in eastern Uganda, there are mountains. But my village here in northern Uganda is flat. It's busy, and there are markets with lots of people selling things.

MY FAMILY

We have a small family. I live with my mother, my uncle and my two sisters – ages seven and three. I'm the oldest. My father works far away in Kampala, the capital of Uganda. My mother runs the best ice-cream business in northern Uganda.

My favourite subjects are maths and science. I like them because they're easy!

Kampala

It's hot in Uganda. Sometimes there is rain. I prefer it when it's raining.

AIMING HIGH

I want to be a pilot when I grow up, so I can fly an aeroplane and go to other countries.

TIME WITH FRIENDS

I like playing outside with my friends, running and riding bicycles. I like sharing with my friends.

NOTHING BUT NET

I play netball with my friends, and I like to score goals. Netball is popular here. Lots of people like to play.

FAVOURITE ANIMAL

My favourite animal is a cow because they give us meat and milk.

MY HOME

My house is on the edge of town, surrounded by fields. I like where we live. It's a quiet home.

Fast Fact: Conflict wrecked Uganda for years, but it ended, and life is slowly improving. Recently, war in neighbouring South Sudan forced more than a million people to flee into northern Uganda. War Child works with families from both countries to rebuild their lives. For example, War Child provided Esther's mother with tools and support to start her ice-cream business.

Ireland

ETHAN
Age 8

My name is Ethan.
I live in Waterford, Ireland.

WATERFORD

We have a river running through Waterford. The bridge going into the city is raised when big ships need to go through. We have lots of beaches, fields for all the farmers and mountains with a small waterfall. There are loads of people around.

MY FAMILY

My family is really big. I have my mum and dad, four uncles and two aunts. I am also lucky to have one great-grandad, one great-grandmother, three nanas and one grandad. I also have a younger sister. I love helping my dad cook dinner. He is a chef and is the best. I love my mum's library. She has loads and loads of books.

MY THREE WORDS
Fun, Smart, Caring

IRISH SCHOOL

I have to go to a *gaelscoil*, which is a school where I have to speak Irish instead of English all the time – even in the playground and at playtime.

Waterford

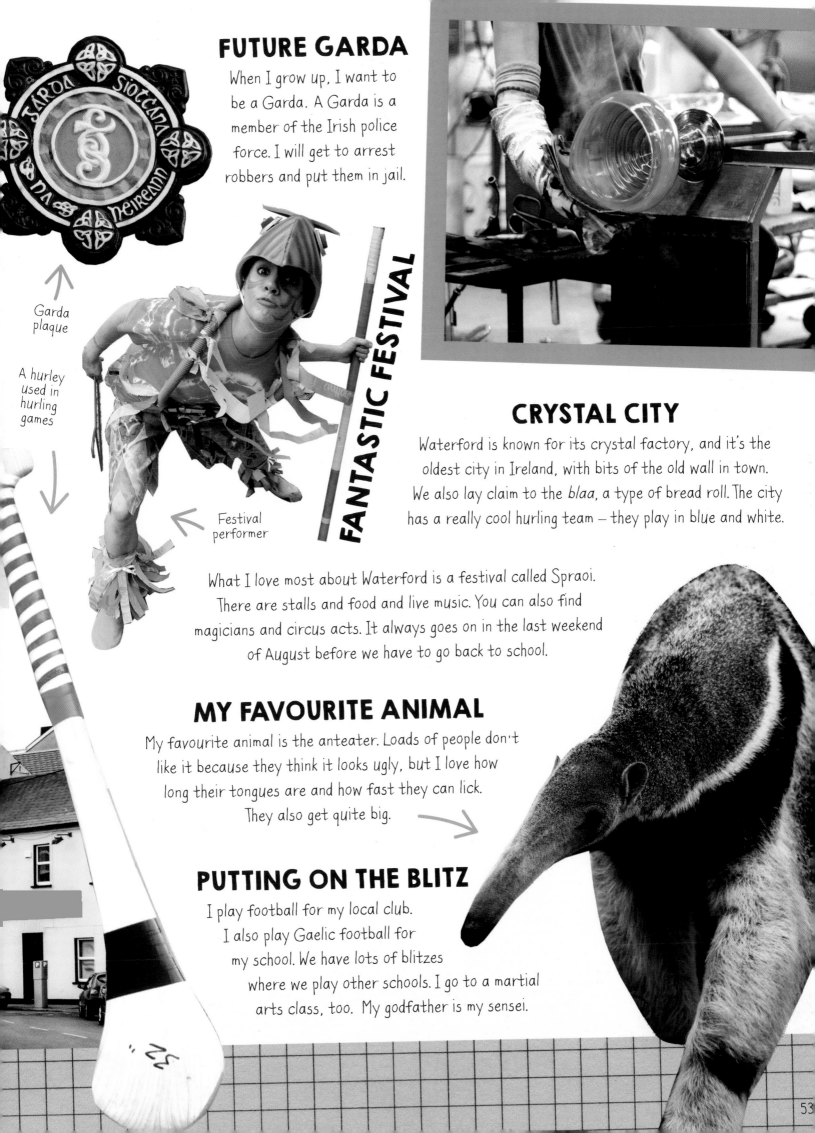

FUTURE GARDA

When I grow up, I want to be a Garda. A Garda is a member of the Irish police force. I will get to arrest robbers and put them in jail.

Garda plaque

A hurley used in hurling games

Festival performer

FANTASTIC FESTIVAL

CRYSTAL CITY

Waterford is known for its crystal factory, and it's the oldest city in Ireland, with bits of the old wall in town. We also lay claim to the *blaa*, a type of bread roll. The city has a really cool hurling team — they play in blue and white.

What I love most about Waterford is a festival called Spraoi. There are stalls and food and live music. You can also find magicians and circus acts. It always goes on in the last weekend of August before we have to go back to school.

MY FAVOURITE ANIMAL

My favourite animal is the anteater. Loads of people don't like it because they think it looks ugly, but I love how long their tongues are and how fast they can lick. They also get quite big.

PUTTING ON THE BLITZ

I play football for my local club. I also play Gaelic football for my school. We have lots of blitzes where we play other schools. I go to a martial arts class, too. My godfather is my sensei.

53

Spain

GAIA
Age 10

My name is Gaia.
I live in Barcelona, Spain.

BARCELONA

My neighbourhood is called Poblenou. It used to be an industrial area with a little town that is now part of Barcelona. I live right in the centre of the neighbourhood, so there are lots of shops and restaurants.

MY FAMILY

My family is quite big and different. I live with my mum, my stepdad and my two younger sisters — Moa and Lila. I also have my cousins Enzo and Leo, and I love them like brothers. My dad lives in another town called Zaragoza with his own family — including my little brother Liam — but I don't see them a lot.

CREATIVE HOBBIES

I like reading! I actually love reading. I also like to listen to music and invent dances with my friends.

I would love to have a cat, or a unicorn!! as a pet.

DIVE IN

I love swimming and snorkelling, and I am not afraid of deep water.

SUN-SOAKED DAYS

Barcelona has Mediterranean weather. It does not rain a lot. We have a lot of sunny days, and in the summer, it gets sooo hot! In the winter, it gets cold for us, but it is very strange to see snow. I've only seen it once in my life.

DREAM IT... DO IT!

I would like to be an actress, a writer or a marine biologist. I love the sea, and my mum wants me to save the sea and the planet!

AFTER SCHOOL

Lots of times after we finish school, we meet outside at the park. We like skating and going on bikes, scooters and skateboards.

SO MUCH TO SEE

Barcelona is known for beaches, festivals, important buildings and museums like the Miro and Picasso. People like to eat out a lot and love getting together. The whole family goes out and stays up later than in other countries. That's the Mediterranean lifestyle!

Barcelona

South Africa

GEMMA
Age 11

My name is Gemma, and I live in Hoedspruit, South Africa.

MY THREE WORDS
Kind, Loving, Adventurous

HOEDSPRUIT

Where I live, the landscape is beautiful, and we are able to view the Drakensberg mountain range. I love that there are a lot of wildlife reserves. We are blessed with a lot of green trees around us.

MY FAMILY

My immediate family is small. I have a dad who works in the air force and my mum is in teaching. My sister is in high school. As a family, we go on frequent walks and enjoy the old traditional *braai* (barbecue) over the weekend.

MY HOUSE

We live in a house that is big enough for a family of four. There are a lot of pictures hanging on the walls. My mum loves pictures. We also have a lovely back garden for our two dogs.

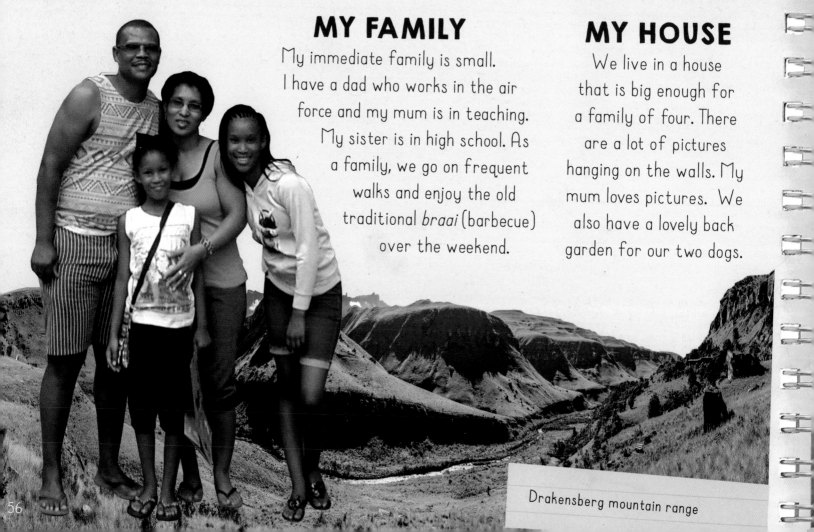

Drakensberg mountain range

NATURE'S CLASSROOM

I like my school, especially because it's nature based. Sometimes while we sit in class, we can see the monkeys, baboons and warthogs. We are so fortunate to have lessons in the bush. It's just AWESOME!

CHARMED BY SNAKES

Due to where I live, I have a few favourite animals. Among them are snakes, wild dogs and elephants.

DREAM TRIP

I would love to go to Switzerland because I am a big fan of chocolate.

WILD PARK

My favourite place that I've visited is the Kruger National Park in northeastern South Africa. The first time I visited, I went there with my family. We saw a lot of animals and made a lot of memories, too.

TOP SPORTS

My favourite sports are hockey, netball and cricket.

Cricket bat and ball

NASIONALE KRUGERWILDTUIN

ORPEN

KRUGER NATIONAL PARK

Kyrgyzstan

GERDA
Age 10

My name is Gerda.
I live in Bishkek, Kyrgyzstan.

MY THREE WORDS

CREATIVE
NATURAL
AMBITIOUS

KYRGYZSTAN

I like that Kyrgyzstan is gorgeous.
Bishkek city – where I live – is
surrounded by snow-capped
mountains. The evergreen trees smell
so nice, and the scent of those trees
moves along with the wind.

The main square in Bishkek

MY FAMILY

My family is neither small nor big. I have my mum, grandma and grandpa. I like doing fun stuff with my mum like going to a park, rope climbing, shopping and watching movies.

Autumn is my favourite season because trees turn different colours, and my birthday is in November.

MY BFF

My best friend's name is Nazima. When we are together, we are like two monkeys because we laugh and giggle a lot. Even when I get mad at her, after a few minutes I just can't help it and I start talking to her again.

My favourite animal is a giraffe because it is very tall and cute.

SLIME!

In my free time, I like making slime and playing with it, or watching my favourite TV shows.

SCHOOL TIME

My favourite subjects are geography, English and PE. The reason I like geography is because I am interested in the mysteries of our Earth.

Most Prized Possessions

I like playing with my Beanie Boos™. They are soft, fluffy and have big cute sparkly eyes. I have collected 44 of them.

Thailand

GYA

AGE
9

My name is Gya.
I live in Bangkok, Thailand.

Fast Fact:
Bangkok is one of the most visited cities in the world. Its landmarks include a 32-storey building shaped like an elephant.

BANGKOK

I live in Bangkok — a city filled with skyscrapers and busy roads. It is rather loud here, and the city is filled with lots of people rushing out of buildings. It's not scorching hot where I live, but it is quite warm!

FAMILY

In my family, there are six people — Mum, Dad, my sister, two brothers and me. My dad is a businessman, and my mum runs a Pilates studio. The children were born: girl, boy, girl and boy. Our ages are: nine, seven, five and one.

MY THREE WORDS
Enthusiastic
Outgoing
Friendly

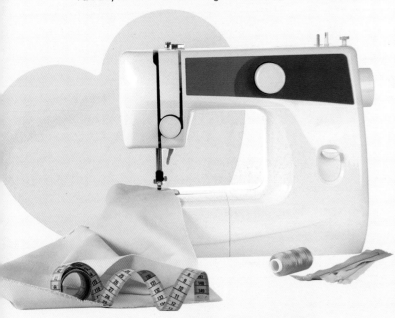

DESIGN BY ME

In school, my favourite subjects are French and design and technology. I want to become a fashion designer because I like sketching new ideas, and I like using a sewing machine.

MY HOME

I live on the top floor of a hotel. I like the breathtaking view at dawn and sunset, but when it rains, we can hear the rain falling fiercely on the windows.

GAME NIGHT

My favourite board game is Monopoly™. My siblings and I quarrel quite often about the rules of the game, but we mostly sort it out in the end.

MY FAVOURITE ANIMAL
Dogs, especially corgis and pugs!

FEELING SPORTY

I like doing gymnastics, swimming and playing T-ball. In my country, football is the most popular sport.

61

Zimbabwe

HAYDEN
AGE 7

My name is Hayden.
I live in Victoria Falls,
Zimbabwe.

MY THREE WORDS
SMART
FUNNY
NAUGHTY

VICTORIA FALLS

In Victoria Falls, the weather is normally very hot and dry except for the rainy season. We never get snow ever. I like to explore outside. I find bones, fossils and new flowers.

MY FAMILY

My family is very small but sometimes very fun. My dad works at Wilderness Safaris and goes into the bush a lot. My mum is from America and likes the computer and reading books. My dad plays with me lots — swimming, cricket and kicking the ball.

CLOSE TO NATURE

People in Victoria Falls like to have fun. We are known for the area's beauty and our famous waterfall. It is very natural here, and lots of things aren't man-made. I love playing in the river and climbing trees.

BORN TO RUN

Track and field is by far
my favourite sport.
I like the 100 metre,
200 metre, high jump and long
jump. It feels good to run.

MY HOME

At my house, it is very quiet except when I am
there! It is very green with lots of trees. I have
a big jungle in my garden. Around us are lots
of bush and animals like elephants, baboons,
warthogs, buffalo, hyenas and lions.

DOG BALL

I like playing rugby
with my biggest dog,
Beaudy, and football
with my little
dog, Lily.

HOP ON!

Where I live is so beautiful. I can ride my motorbike
anywhere. I love to ride my motorbike and shoot my
pellet gun at empty tins. I am a very good shot!

Austria

HELENA
AGE 9

My name is Helena. I live in Stadlau, Austria.

STADLAU

We live close to a lake in Stadlau, a suburb of Vienna — the capital of Austria. People around me like to play sport and work outside in their gardens.

FAMILY

We are a small family — just Mum, Dad, my older sister, Lea, and our cat, Fredi. My parents both work during the day and are only at home in the evening. I sometimes fight with my sister, but we also play a lot of sport together and have fun.

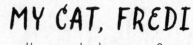

MY CAT, FREDI

I love all animals, but my favourite animal is a cat! A cat is a perfect pet as it is not so much work.

BUILDING MEMORIES

My mum, sister and I went with some friends to Legoland® in Germany. Legoland® is similar to Disney World® — a park with rollercoasters and many things to discover. We had so much fun!

Lea and me at Legoland®

DRAMA LOVER

I want to become an actress. I already had a role in a movie. It was great fun.

YEAR-ROUND FUN

We have great mountains where we can go walking and climbing in the summer and skiing in the winter. I love winter because my birthday is at the end of the winter season!

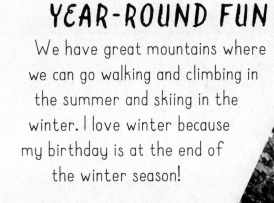

FAST HORSE

When I ride a horse, I like when we are outside in the field or forest. I also like when we canter and go very fast!

TEAM PLAYER

I like playing sport — especially hockey, vaulting and riding. Hockey is my favourite sport, as it is great to play on a team.

Guyana

IKIE

AGE 11

My name is Ikie.
I live in Surama, North
Rupununi Region 9
in Guyana.

MY THREE WORDS
Handsome, Chubby, Smart

MY FAMILY

In my family, I have two brothers, my
mum, my dad and myself. My parents
are both tour guides and drivers.
We live in a house. It has two bedrooms
—one which my brothers and I sleep in
and the other for my mum and dad.

SURAMA

Surama is a village surrounded by mountains and
savanna (grassland). We do not live by the sea, but
we have an airstrip, where tourists can come into.
Our market days are at the end of the month, and
we also have a clinic day on the last Wednesday of
the month to help the sick.

FEEL THE HEAT

Sometimes it rains a lot, and sometimes it can be so hot that we do not go out. We do not have snow, but that would be cool because I've never seen snow.

FIRST PEOPLE

I am an indigenous boy, and my people are the Macushi tribe — the first people to live in Guyana. Our community welcomes tourists to our village.

Auntie making cassava bread

FREE TIME

I like to play with my toy soldiers in the sand and ride my bike around the village. I would like to become a soldier.

HOLIDAY

We took a trip to Georgetown — Guyana's capital — to experience one of our national holidays called Republic Day.

THE FARM

In my community, we like to go on the farm to clean and plant cassava (yucca) and other plants to feed our family.

WILD TIME

The best adventure my friends and I ever had was swimming in a pond with a caiman. We did not know it was there until it poked its head out, and we all got out the water as fast as we could!

Caiman

Lithuania

ILJA
AGE 7

My name is Ilja. I live in Klaipėda, Lithuania.

MY THREE WORDS

BOY, SWIMMER, ROBOTICS-LOVER

KLAIPĖDA

Klaipėda is situated by the Baltic Sea. We have a beach and a big port. There are also forests and parks, theatres and museums. People in Klaipėda speak different languages: Lithuanian, Russian and English.

MY FAMILY

In my family, there is my mother and my father, my sister, Aliona, two grandmothers and two grandfathers. My father is a sailor. My mother used to work as a hairdresser, but now she looks after the household and my little sister who is two.

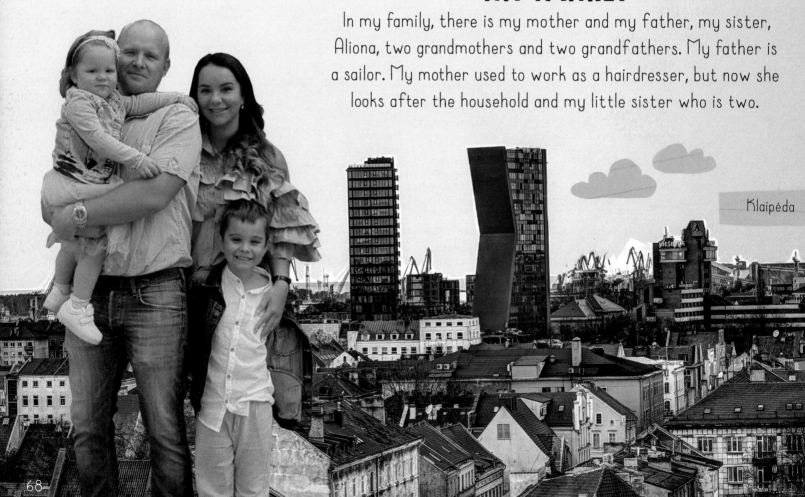

Klaipėda

MY HOME

We live in a flat with three rooms, as well as a bathroom, a kitchen and a balcony. It is on the ninth floor – the top floor of our building.

SEA CELEBRATION

Every summer there is a sea festival here. People can see the sailing boats that come to Klaipėda from all over the world! There are many concerts, performances and a big fireworks display.

GET ACTIVE

I like swimming, badminton and jumping on the trampoline, but in Lithuania, the most popular sport is basketball.

COOL CREATIONS

I like drawing, colouring and going to robotics classes where we learn to build robots and other things.

SUMMER FUN

We like to go to our *dacha* (summer house) outside Klaipėda, where we relax and have barbecues. I like to build things with my father. We built a playhouse and a sandpit for my little sister at the *dacha*.

MY SCHOOL

At school, I like PE and learning the Lithuanian language. I don't like maths and reading because there is just too much to do! I want to be an engineer, an architect or a builder. I also want to have a shop and sell Lego™.

Fiji

JACK
Age 8

My name is Jack.
I live in Nadi, Fiji.

NADI

Nadi is a farming community. My family and I live outside of town. The road to my house from the main road is a track and can be dusty, but there is also a nice breeze.

MY FAMILY

I have a small family. There is my dad, my brother and my sister. My dad works for an island resort. I love my brother, Joe, because he plays with me and rides bikes with me. I love my sister, Contina, because she looks after me.

MY FAVOURITE ANIMAL

I like the lion because he is powerful, strong and the king of the jungle. There are no lions in Fiji, but I wish I could see one. I see lions on TV shows, and they scare me with how fast they run, how they fight and how big they are.

MY THREE WORDS **FOOD-LOVER** **PLAYFUL** **HAPPY**

ZIP LINE

I loved visiting the Sabeto zip line near the Sleeping Giant mountain range. We had to walk up a jungle path. I felt like I was in a movie as it didn't feel like I was in Fiji. We zip-lined down and ended up swimming in clean, cool waterfalls.

STORM WARNING

I hope there are no hurricanes this year. This year there are a lot of mangoes, and people say that lots of mangoes means a hurricane is coming. I hope they are wrong.

FARM LIFE

There are lots of cows and horses around that belong to my neighbours. When I am standing in my front garden, I see farms, a big pond and lots of open space that is used for vegetable or sugar cane farming.

MOVES LIKE MESSI

Popular sports in Fiji are rugby and football. I love playing football because I want to be like Lionel Messi and do fancy tricks. I don't play with football boots, but I still enjoy the game and scoring goals.

GONE FISHING

Where I live, there is a big pond that is full of fish. People come from the highlands to fish in that pond. It's covered with water lilies.

Guatemala

JAVIER
Age 10

Antigua Ruins

My name is Javier. I live in Santa Lucia Milpas Altas, Guatemala.

MY THREE WORDS

Fun

Curious

Collaborator

SANTA LUCIA MILPAS ALTAS

Santa Lucia Milpas Altas is in the mountains — a nice place and very green. We're close to a popular city called Antigua. We go there for the market and to visit my grandparents. Antigua was the capital of Guatemala a long time ago.

MY FAMILY

My family is small. I am an only child, but I have cousins and they live close to me. They are like my brothers. My papa is Alex. He works with foreign volunteers. Sometimes they visit our house, and I can talk with them. My mama's name is Mirsa. She is a teacher.

LAND OF VOLCANOES

We have many volcanoes in Guatemala. I want to go with my father to the mountains and hike a volcano.

My family

IN BLOOM

Where I live, there are many flower shops and wooden-furniture stores. It is beautiful because people like to have flowers.

GUATEMALAN BREAKFAST

MY HOME

My house is very nice. I love to be there. My room is on the first floor. I like to play in the garden and eat. In the morning, I can see birds — yellow, blue and other colours. I also see hummingbirds.

MY FAVOURITE CLASS

In my school, we have a class called robotica. We build electronic items with old things. We made a personal battery fan, and we also built a little toy car.

JUNIOR CHEF

I like cooking different things such as pizza, pancakes and the traditional breakfast from Guatemala.

FEELING CRAFTY

I like to learn how to do crafts that I see on YouTube or in magazines.

JAYLYNN
AGE 9

My name is Jaylynn. I live
in Thomasburg, Ontario, Canada.

MY THREE WORDS
SMART, STRONG, HELPFUL

THOMASBURG

We live in Thomasburg, about an hour away from
the city of Kingston. We have a lot of space. I can
ride my bike all over the garden, and I know my
next-door neighbours. They are so friendly and nice. There
are not a lot of new people who come around,
so we know almost everyone.

MY FAMILY

I am an only child, and I have a big family that is always
there to support me and love me. My mom is a nurse,
and my dad works in a factory. My stepdad works with
heating and air-conditioning. My aunt and grandma work
at a Sears department store.

Kingston

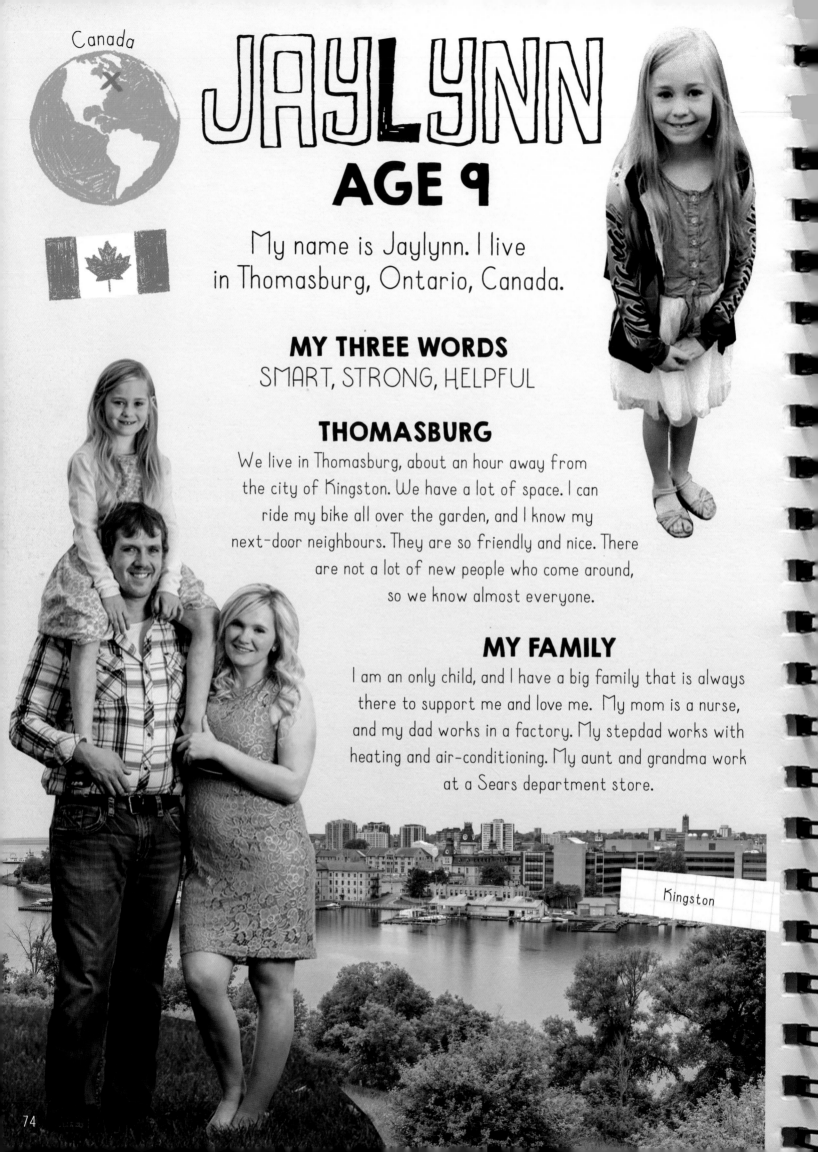

NEW SCHOOL

I changed schools this year. A lot of my friends are at my old school, and some have moved away. I am starting a French language immersion course, so I am making new friends.

MONSTER-SIZED FUN

My friends love coming over for our Halloween parties every year. We get to dress up and play games.

CHEER SQUAD

I love cheerleading. I cheer in Kingston twice a week for two hours, and I tumble twice a week for about an hour. It's a lot of work, but I wouldn't change it. I appreciate all my parents do for me. I have a few friends who want to play sport, but they can't, so I am thankful that I am able to.

MY HOME

I live in a four-bedroom bungalow when I am with my mum, and we have a garage where I store my bikes, helmets and fishing poles. I live in my father's house when I am staying with him.

I like four-wheeling, fishing, skiing and boat rides.

Nepal

JENISHA
AGE 8

My name is Jenisha.
I live in Kathmandu, Nepal.

KATHMANDU

Kathmandu is in a valley with the
Himalaya mountain range to the
north, but we can only see the
mountains on a clear day. We live
in a densely populated city —
almost 5 million people. It's
very busy, but it's quiet at
night-time.

Fast Fact: Nepal
is the only country
in the world with a
national flag that is
not a rectangle.

MY FAMILY

In my family, I have an
older sister, a younger
brother, Mum and Dad.
I also have two uncles
and one aunt who live
in our house. We live in
a big house with many
bedrooms for all of us.
My dad tells us we are very
fortunate to have all these.

MANY SEASONS

We have six seasons —
one every two months. During
monsoon season it rains a lot.
In the winter, it doesn't snow
in the valley, but gets cold.
Summers are hot.

Fast Fact: Mount Everest,
part of the Himalaya
mountain range, is the
world's tallest mountain
at 8,848 m (29,029 feet).
In Nepali, it is called
Sagarmatha — meaning
'goddess of the sky' or
'forehead in the sky'.

SO MUCH TO CELEBRATE

Kathmandu is very diverse, with many people of different ethnicities, cultures and languages. The city has many festivals where different community groups celebrate.

JUST FOR FUN

I love drawing and sketching, riding bikes and doing creative things. We go to visit around town and other places when Dad has days off.

NATURE DAYS

Visiting our grandparents in their cabin in the village is fun because it's all in nature.

I LIKE PLAYING GAMES ON MY IPAD® AND WATCHING TV.

OFF TO SCHOOL

My sister and I go to an all-girls' school in Kathmandu. We have to get up early to get ready and catch the school bus by 8:00 a.m. Because of traffic, the ride takes a long time. We get to school by 9:00-9:30 a.m.

My School Uniform

Trinidad and Tobago

JORDAN
Age 9

MY THREE WORDS
ACTIVE
STUBBORN
MISCHIEVOUS

My name is Jordan. I live in Tunapuna, Trinidad and Tobago.

TUNAPUNA

Tunapuna is in the foothills of the Northern Range in Trinidad. Neighbours live very close together, but the area is generally quiet. Some of the families in my community have lived here for many generations, just like my father's family.

MY FAMILY

I have one sister and a mother and father. We all live together with my grandmother. I fight a lot with my sister. She likes to boss me around because she is older, but I miss her when she is not around.

HOMESCHOOLER

I am homeschooled by my mum, who works from home. When my mum has to travel sometimes for work, my sister and I go with her and it is like a field trip and learning experience.

TROPICAL TEMPS

The temperature is always hot. We live in the tropics, so there are only two seasons — the rainy season and the dry season.

CARNIVAL

Carnival in Trinidad and Tobago is a pre-Lenten celebration. Kiddie's Carnival — the children's carnival — is celebrated two weekends before the adult parades. Hundreds of children dressed in costumes parade through the streets in cities and towns.

Carnival Costume

Tunapuna is known for steel pan during Carnival time.

MY HOME

I live in a concrete bungalow. There are three bedrooms. I like to help doing work in the garden like mowing and raking up the grass. I also like to water the plants and wash down the drains.

WELL-BALANCED

My sister and I love doing stilt walking for fun. I can balance on one leg when I am wearing my stilts. I hope to graduate to 0.9-m (3-foot) stilts soon.

Fast Fact:
Stilt walking is an African tradition that was brought to Trinidad and Tobago. Stilt walkers and dancers (also called *moko jumbies*) are a common sight during Carnival and are included in other celebrations during the year.

Czech Republic

JULIE AGE 9

My name is Julie. I live in Rajhradice, Czech Republic.

RAJHRADICE

My home is in a small village called Rajhradice which lies near the city of Brno. There are about 1,200 people in my village. Our landscape is very flat, and there are a lot of fields with wheat, corn, sunflowers and potatoes.

MY FAMILY

My brother, Kryštof, is five years old. Although I have only one brother, my family is big. This is because I have eight cousins. My grandmother lives with us in our house, so it is always a big event when they all come to visit.

MY THREE WORDS

CLEVER

NICE

PRETTY

MY SCHOOL

Although I am not very good at reading, I like literature class because we have a very nice teacher. I also like English. I don't like the Czech language because it is boring.

NEW BEDROOM

We live in a two-storey house. I share a bedroom with my brother, but I will get my own bedroom on my tenth birthday. I'm already planning how it will look. I want wooden or white furniture and brightly coloured accessories.

OLD TRADITION

In the spring, we have a traditional feast. Young boys and girls wear folk costumes and dance and sing throughout the village.

HANDMADE

Last year, I learned to knit. I knitted winter hats for all my family and friends.

MY FAVOURITE ANIMAL

Dogs—especially our seven-month-old puppy who is named Dorotka.

SWIM AND SKATE

In the summer, we go to a swimming pool or to a pond in our village. In the winter, when the pond is frozen, we go skating there. We are lucky to have snow in the winter.

Rajhradice

KAARLO
AGE 9

My name is Kaarlo. I live in Helsinki, Finland.

HELSINKI

Helsinki is the biggest city in Finland, but our neighbourhood is in the suburbs. There is a lot of nature around.

MY FAMILY

My family is Mum, Dad, me and my two little brothers. Pietari is seven years old and Ruben is three. We do fight every now and then, but I still love them, as they are good playmates, and I can turn to them for advice.

SUPER SUMMERS...
SOMETIMES

Finland is known for cold winters. Summers are sometimes hot and fantastic. Too bad it doesn't happen every year!

MY THREE WORDS

Fair
Nice
Friendly

TOP SPORTS

Floorball (floor hockey) is quite popular around here. Football is, too.

SCHOOL TIME

My favourite subjects are sports, maths and music. I like the games we play in sports classes, and I like solving mathematical problems. Our teacher is very musically oriented, so we get to do a lot of band stuff during music lessons. My least favourite subject is Finnish. It's boring.

MY FAVOURITE ANIMAL

Dog. No question. I put in a lot of effort to convince my parents to get a dog.

Playing with my uncle's dog, Taro

I like Finnish Christmas traditions. Santa Claus lives in Finland, you know?

MY HOBBIES

My hobbies are parkour, playing the piano and practising chess. Some new hobbies could be fun!

KAYA
AGE 7

My name is Kaya.
I live in Messery, France.

MESSERY

I live in Messery, a small village on the southern shore of Lake Geneva in France. Our village is fairly quiet. On Sunday afternoons, it is like a ghost town once the butchers and *boulangeries* (bakeries) have closed!

MY FAMILY

We are five in our family. I am the youngest. My two big brothers, Niko and Mischa, are 16 and 14 years old. My father is German and works across the lake in Geneva, Switzerland. My mother is English and is a travel writer. At home, we speak English, French and German.

MY THREE WORDS
SMILEY, SPORTY, HAPPY

CITY OF LIGHT

My favourite place is Paris because it has lots of beautiful buildings — and Disneyland®! I have been up the Eiffel Tower several times, and each time I find it very exciting to be so high up. It is like being on top of the world. I also love Paris' big shops, bright lights and the Arc de Triomphe.

MY FAVOURITE SHOES

SUMMER

In the summer, everyone is on or by the lake. Messery is known for its pretty, pebbly beach with lots of grass, two wooden jetties to jump from, and stand-up paddleboards to rent.

HORSING AROUND

I am pretty sporty. (You have to be, living here.) My number one sport is horse riding. In France, we do not have school on Wednesdays, so I spend every Wednesday afternoon at the stables.

WINTER

In the winter, I ski every weekend. Both my big brothers race, and I will start racing this winter.

MY BREAKFAST

MERMAID GOALS

I love the lake and the mountains. I sometimes wish I were a mermaid so I could live in the lake and swim all day.

DURA-

Wales

KELSIE
AGE 11

My name is Kelsie.
I live in Colwyn Bay,
Wales, in the United Kingdom.

MY THREE WORDS

Weird
Intelligent
Kind

COLWYN BAY

The weather in Colwyn Bay is a mix. Sometimes it rains. Sometimes it's sunny, but it hardly ever snows. Because we're higher up in altitude than everyone else in the area, the weather we get is stronger.

MY FAMILY

In my family there is me, my mum, my stepdad, my dad, my brother and my grandma. My mum is a registered residential manager, my stepdad is a Royal Air Force engineer, and my dad is a submariner for the Royal Navy. My little brother is named Thomas. He is nearly three.

BEAUTIFUL BEACHES

We live near Anglesey — an island off the northwest coast of Wales. I love the beaches there and in Colwyn Bay.

Colwyn Bay

CHARITY BAKE SALE

I have Tourette's syndrome, and this year we did a bake sale with my school for the charity Tourettes Action and raised over £65!

WALK IN THE WOODS

The environment is lovely in Colwyn Bay. I live near the woods, which is fun for walking.

STRIKING A CHORD

I am learning the guitar, and I am pretty advanced.

BOOK LOVER

I like reading a lot. I play a make-believe game where I'm Hermione Granger, and that I attend Hogwarts.

MAD FOR MANCHESTER

My favourite place that I've visited is Manchester. I saw the pop group Little Mix in Manchester Stadium with my mum.

Fast Fact: Wales is home to more than 600 castles. Many were built by foreign invaders!

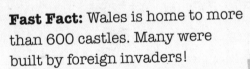

Conwy Castle in Wales

Jamaica

KITARA
AGE 7

My name is Kitara. I live in Kingston, Jamaica.

KINGSTON

Jamaica is very hilly. The weather is mostly hot and sunny. It gets really hot during the summer and a little cooler during the winter, but it never snows because Jamaica is a tropical island.

MY FAMILY

I have a tiny family. I wish I had a little brother or sister, but it's just me, my mummy and my daddy. Even though my immediate family is tiny, I have a huge extended family. My mummy is an only child like me, but my nana has 11 siblings and my grandpa has 10 siblings!

OUT IN SPACE

When I grow up, I want to be an astronomer, astrophysicist or engineer. I'm going to travel to outer space to explore our solar system. I loooove learning about our solar system.

MY FRUIT TREES

I live in a community with over 200 townhouses. My house has lots of fruit trees outside. There is a cherry tree, coconut tree, sweetsop tree, ackee tree and two mango trees. Sweetsop is my favourite fruit. I also love ackee cooked with saltfish. That's Jamaica's national dish.

Sweetsop

LABOUR DAY

On 23 May every year, we celebrate Labour Day in Jamaica by beautifying and helping our communities. In my community, we sweep the car park, paint the parking spaces and paint the walls and pavements. Last year, the kids helped with the painting, and then we got to play in a bouncy castle and an inflatable pool.

CITY TRAFFIC

Kingston is very busy, and there is a lot of traffic. My friend Taylor takes over an hour to get to school if she doesn't leave home at 6:30 a.m. Luckily, I don't spend a lot of time in traffic because I live close to my school and places where I do other activities.

SUNNY FUN

When it's sunny, I like to go swimming with my friends.

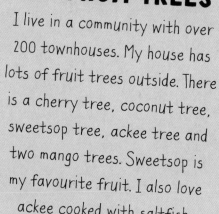

I love that my daddy makes go-karts with me.

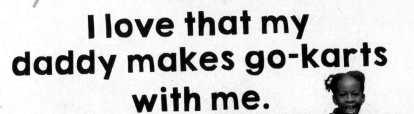

Malawi

KUMBUKANI
AGE 11

My name is Kumbukani, and I live in Nandumbo, Balaka District, Malawi.

NANDUMBO

I am part of the Lomwe tribe, but we live in a Yao tribe community called Nandumbo because my father works there. There are so many annual festivals with dancing and singing. Houses are built in groups as families that then make up larger communities. Large pieces of land are left for farming.

MY FAMILY

There are six people in my family – Dad, Mum, my three sisters and me. My father works in a national park.

FARM TO TABLE

I like spending time farming with my mother whenever I am on school holiday. We grow a lot of maize, peas, Irish potatoes and tomatoes. We eat a lot from our own gardens, so we buy less food.

WHAT'S COOKING?

We eat maize meal (cornmeal) and a lot of fish.

My Mum

MY SCHOOL

The most beautiful building in our community is our school. We have eight classrooms, a playground, a library and rainwater harvesting tanks. I love it so much. My favourite subject is English. My least favourite subject is Chichewa, the local language.

ANIMAL DOCTOR

I love elephants, and I would like to become a vet. I have always admired the veterinarians who fly into the national park and treat the animals.

GOOD GAME

I like playing football. I play on a junior team at our school as one of the strikers. The game makes me feel good.

ELEPHANT CROSSING

We live in a house with three bedrooms, very close to Liwonde National Park. There a lot of trees and wild animals. Sometimes we hide inside our house when we see elephants nearby, but we all love wildlife.

Kenya

KWAMBOKA
Age 6

My name is Kwamboka. I live in Lamu Island, Kenya.

LAMU

In Lamu, people are mostly Muslim. They spend their time going to the mosque and the beach, too. You can play sport at the beach, such as surfing and windsurfing.

MY FAMILY

My family is small. It's me and my mum. We like going to the pool to swim and throw each other in the water. My mum works at Safari Doctors. She helps people and gives them medicine.

MY THREE WORDS

CREATIVE

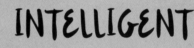
INTELLIGENT

BLACK-GIRL

BEACH DAY

At the beach, you can make sand balls. You take wet sand, then you shape it into a ball, put dry sand on top, then keep adding until it feels like a rock. You throw it in the ocean, and it makes a big PLOP noise!

SAFARI DOCTORS

Once I went on a trip with my mum and Safari Doctors. I learned about blood pressure, and I had a small operation done by the dentist there on my teeth. When I got home, another tooth was wobbly, so I pulled it out myself. I lost two teeth in one day!

TURTLE TROUBLE

My best adventure was when I went to find turtles at my friend's house — until I got into trouble because I didn't tell anyone I was going there! I was given a time out for that.

MY FAVOURITE GAME

Sometimes my friends and I play games outside of school. Our favourite game is Fanta-Coca-Cola. It's like hide-and-seek.

RETURN TO ENGLAND

I would like to visit England because I was born there. I'd like to go back now that I'm older, so I can understand the games they play there, and go to places I haven't been.

HOLIDAY TIME

People in Lamu spend a lot of time with their families at Eid al-Fitr.

Fast Fact: Eid al-Fitr is a religious holiday celebrated by Muslims. It marks the end of the holy month of Ramadan.

Chile

LAURA
AGE 9

MY THREE WORDS

CREATIVE

NICE

FUNNY

My name is Laura. I live in Puerto Varas, Chile.

PUERTO VARAS

In Puerto Varas, the climate changes a lot. It is cold in the autumn, and it rains a lot during the winter, autumn and spring. Summer is hotter. There is snow on the volcanoes during all seasons.

MY FAMILY

In my family it's my father, my mother, my younger sister, Blanca, and me. My father is a birdwatching guide. My mother works in an office. We like to watch movies and travel.

MY VIEW

Puerto Varas is very green, with a huge lake. From my window, I can see the whole city, the church and many houses like mine. I also like to see the volcanoes.

Puerto Varas

MY HOUSE

My house is not very big, but it is big enough for the number of people who live in it. My sister and I have our rooms on the first floor. We share the space with our pet — a small Chinese hamster named Melón.

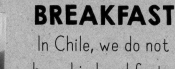

BREAKFAST

In Chile, we do not have big breakfasts. I drink chocolate milk and eat bread known as *hallula*. We often have it with avocado, apricot, berry marmalade or butter.

LOL

As a joke, I like to put toothpaste on biscuits for my family!

HOW WE ROLL

I like to play video games, but I like any game with my friends more. We roller skate and climb, and we also make construction projects and gear using different materials.

DREAM TRIP

I would like to visit Italy because my father lived and studied there, and my grandparents were born there.

Favourite animal

ARCTIC FOX

United States

LEO
Age 9

My name is Leo.
I live in Barrow,
Alaska, USA.

BARROW

Barrow is flat, treeless and covered in snow six months of the year. We live at the top of Alaska, and it's colder than most places! I love the crisp, cold fresh air. There are about 4,500 people in Barrow. We have nearby villages that are not accessible by roads.

A TRADITIONAL WHALING COMMUNITY

We live in the Arctic where permafrost (frozen ground) prevents any trees, crops or gardens from growing. We say the ocean is our garden since we hunt and eat the bowhead whales, beluga whales, seals, walruses and fish. We also eat a lot of caribou, ducks and geese.

NATIVE DANCING

We have a strong tradition of Iñupiaq dancing. Some dances tell stories with words and motions while others are just motion dances. At the annual Alaska Federation of Natives convention, I performed with my uncle, my brother Andrew, my mother, my stepfather and my sister Kivvaq.

My etching

MY FAVOURITE ANIMAL

My favourite animal is the wolverine because they are so strong. They can take down many animals. They are fierce.

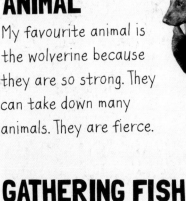

GATHERING FISH

For a few weeks a year, small fish wash up and we gather these. We give a lot of them to the elders who aren't able to catch fish anymore.

TWO CREWS

I am on two whaling crews. My father has a whaling crew, Akootchook Crew, and my mother is in her husband's family whaling crew, the Patkotak Crew. There are two whaling seasons, spring and autumn. I made an etching on the baleen of a bowhead whale.

OUTDOOR FUN

We play outside all year long. In the summer, we jump on homemade seesaws. It's a lot of fun to see how high we can jump. In the winter, we play out in the snow — snowball fights, building snow forts, and snow machine rides. I also like to play video games on my Playstation 4™.

We like to go ice fishing.

Israel

LIORA
Age 9

My name is Liora, and I live in Zichron Yaakov, Israel.

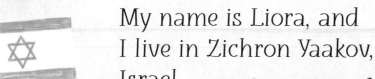

MY THREE WORDS
Creative

Energetic

Reader

ZICHRON YAAKOV

We live quite close to the Mediterranean Sea, and we can see it from the windows of our house. It's very quiet except for dogs barking, but when we go onto the main road, there are lots of people, and lots of cats. I like to name them!

MY FAMILY

My family includes my little sister, Rina, my big half-sister, Joelle, my dad, Marc, and my mum, Ruth. Joel is away at college. Our family is quit small, but we see a lot of my grandm and grandpa who also live in Zichro My other grandma lives in Spain, an she comes to visit sometimes.

My bedroom

UPSTAIRS, DOWNSTAIRS

We live in a house with two floors. We have bedrooms upstairs, but my sister and I like to sleep downstairs on the sofas. We only really use our bedrooms as a place for our clothes and for doing our projects and colouring.

ART ALL AROUND

I like drawing and photography. I take photos of the beautiful sunsets we have here.

NEW BELT

Krav Maga is a way of moving and kicking and doing active things so you can protect yourself if someone tries to hurt you. I now have an orange-green belt.

CAFÉ BREAK

There are a lot of wineries and vineyards near where I live, so people like to sit in cafés and have wine, coffee, breakfast and things like that. When I'm going to school, I see a lot of farmland and vineyards from the car.

FAMILY FUN

In our spare time, my family like going out to the local gardens that are called Ramat Hanadiv. We also spend Shabbat (Friday night to sundown Saturday) together, when we all eat and play games.

Ramat Hanadiv

Costa Rica

LLUVIA
AGE 12

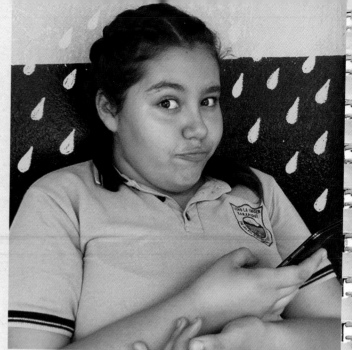

My name is Lluvia.
I live in the Chilamate
Rainforest Eco
Retreat in Sarapiqui,
Costa Rica.

SARAPIQUI

It is very green and hot and humid where I live in
the tropical rainforest. The main attraction in our
area is the Sarapiqui River. The river is cool and
great for kayaking, rafting and swimming. I live in
a small town that is very friendly.

MY FAMILY

There are five of us in my family – Mum
and Dad, my little brother, Aedan, and my
little sister, Kiara. We operate a family-
run conservation project and eco lodge.
I love my little brother and sister, but
they usually drive me nuts!

MY THREE WORDS
SMART, FUNNY, KIND

RAIN NAME

I think everyone in my country knows my
name since it is Lluvia – which means 'rain'.

Kinkajou

MY HOME

My house is part of Chilamate Rainforest Eco Retreat. It is very open and spacious and was built by my dad. Once we had a sloth in our house, and the kinkajou passes through almost every night!

MY FUTURE

I want to do lots of things. I dream of having a rescue centre, owning a restaurant, helping my parents with Chilamate Rainforest Eco Retreat, and being a teacher!

The humidity is high here in the lowland rainforest, so it is important to drink lots of water.

Sloth

ALL WET

Swimming is definitely my favourite sport, and I love walking in the forest. Everyone loves and plays football here except me!

MY FRIENDS ARE SILLY AND FUN. WE LOVE TO HANG OUT, PLAY ON OUR MOBILE PHONES AND TAKE SILLY SELFIES.

South Africa

MACKENZIE
AGE 9

My name is Mackenzie.
I live in Johannesburg,
South Africa.

MY THREE WORDS

Cute

Funny

Happy

JOHANNESBURG

In Johannesburg, South Africa, the weather
is beautiful. It gets very hot, and it mostly
rains in the summer. Where we live, it
is rather flat, but driving farther out of
Johannesburg, it becomes more hilly.

MY FAMILY

There are four people in my
family – my dad, my mum,
my younger sister and me.
My dad is lots of fun. My
sister is animal-crazy. My
mum is happy, and I am
always dancing.

DANCE PARTY

I like to dance and sing.
My dad plays music really
loud, and we all dance around
the table in our lounge.

TEAM PLAYER

I played for a netball team this year and swam for our school swimming team. My favourite stroke is the breaststroke.

AT SCHOOL

My favourite subjects are maths, English, Afrikaans and life skills. When I am older, I would like to be a teacher.

PET FRIENDLY

I love animals. We have a rescue dog called Puppy, two bunnies named Snuggles and Snowflake and two guinea pigs named GP1 and GP2.

FRIENDS AND FUN

My friends and I play in the street of our complex and celebrate holidays together. On Heritage Day, we have a *braai* – a barbecue – and a really huge Slip 'N Slide®.

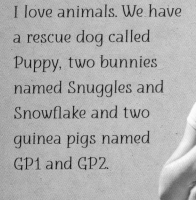

Fast Fact: Held in September, Heritage Day encourages South Africans to celebrate their rich and varied cultural heritage.

SPYING BIG CATS

South Africa's Kruger National Park is one of my favourite places because I love the beautiful animals and getting up early to spot leopards and lions.

India

MANUEL
Age 9

My name is Manuel,
and I live in Goa, India.

GOA

In Goa, it is hot most of the year. Our monsoon season is from June to September, and it rains quite a lot during this time.

MY FAMILY

In my family are my parents, Luis and Chryselle, and my grandmother, Elvira. My father was a doctor but is now in music education. My mother is a writer.

BIG RIVER

We live across from the Mandovi River. It is a very broad river. We have coal-carrying barges (yuck), fishing boats, large on-river casinos and smaller pleasure cruisers. The roads are always busy with traffic and noisy most of the time.

HISTORIC HOUSE

Our house is more than 300 years old and has a lot of history. It was the Royal Mint of Goa (1834-1842). A mint is where coins are made. It has thick walls and a large veranda overlooking the road and the river.

MUSIC ROOM

In our living room, we have music lessons — violin and piano for me. Sometimes we also hold orchestra rehearsals for a music charity for disadvantaged children that my family founded.

DREAM JOB

I want to be an inventor because I build all the time.

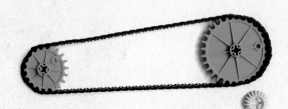

MY FAVOURITE FOODS

My favourite food is pizza. And mangoes. Rice and fish are an important part of our main meals. We also eat vegetables, beef, chicken and other meats.

MY SCHOOL

My school is a boys' school, and it has over 1,000 students. We have a playground, a football pitch, an oratory where we can play indoor games, a basketball court and a shrine to Our Lady of Fatima (an important figure in Catholicism). It is a short four-minute drive from my house.

Goa

Norway

MARI

Age 12

My name is Mari. I live in Lillehammer, Norway.

LILLEHAMMER

Located at the northern end of Lake Mjosa, my town is surrounded by green hills and mountains. In the winter, the town turns white, covered in snow, and the lake freezes to ice.

MY THREE WORDS

Detail-oriented
Funny
Reliable

MY FAMILY

I live with my mother, father and younger brother. My grandfather lives in our town, too. My family is a typically sized Norwegian family. Lots of people think all Norwegians have blue eyes and blonde hair. This is not true. I'm an example!

I have a beautiful view from my room.

In the spring, the days get longer, day by day, until there is hardly any night by May.

OLYMPIC HOST

Lillehammer is a well-known winter sports town. It hosted the Winter Olympic Games in 1994. Where I live, people can go cross-country skiing almost everywhere, both in the forests and in the mountains. There is also a big ski jump in the town.

MY ROOM

I just got my own bedroom. I used to share a room with my brother until this summer. I usually do my homework in my room.

OFF TO SCHOOL

My favourite subjects at school are arts and crafts and food and health. We have our own school iPad® on which we do our homework, and we can use different apps to learn more.

POPULAR SPORTS

I practise football with my team in the summer season, and we play matches once or twice a week. Football, handball, alpine skiing and ice hockey are the most popular sports here.

Brazil

MARINA
AGE 8

My name is Marina.
I live in Brasília, Brazil.

BRASÍLIA

I live in Brasília, the federal capital of Brazil. The city was built in the 1960s, and its architects thought a lot about adding natural spaces near our homes. I wake up listening to birds, and the air is very clean.

MY FAMILY

My family is small. There is my dad, my mum and me. My father works as an IT scientist, and my mother is a journalist. We are very close and work as a team, helping each other all the time. My mother works from home, so she helps me to study, and we do a lot of things together.

PUBLIC EVENTS

We have plenty of public spaces and a long dry season, so we have lots of free events around where I live.

MY THREE WORDS
Friendly, Funny, Tuned-in

BEATING THE HEAT

Brazil is a tropical country. We have hot weather almost the whole year round. At night it gets nice, and we can sleep well if we open our windows. It is almost as if we have natural air-conditioning.

PLAYFUL PETS

I play with my pets a lot. I have three cats — Hermeto Pascoal, Helena Cicy and Letícia Margot. I also have five fish.

NATURAL BEAUTY

In Brasília, there is a huge lake named Paranoá, where people go for a stroll in the late afternoon when the heat is not so strong. Surrounding Brasília, there are lots of waterfalls and beautiful natural places to visit. I love nature!

SCHOOL BAND

I play in my school band, where I have good friends. I play percussion — atabaque, mainly. My band master is tough, but I learn a lot from him.

MY GOALS

I would like to study biology and work for an animal sanctuary.

Atabaque

Bulgaria

MARTINA
AGE 8

My name is Martina.
I live in Sofia, Bulgaria.

MY THREE WORDS
Fun
Happy
Playful

SOFIA
Sofia is the biggest city in Bulgaria. It is busy with a lot of cars, but it also has some nice parks. We live next to the biggest park and enjoy spending time there. I can hear the birds every morning, and it's really beautiful.

MY FAMILY
Our family is big and very connected. I live with Mum and Dad and my sister, Stefania (age six). We spend a lot of time with Aunt and Uncle, my cousin and my grandmas and grandpas. Every week, all of us get together for a family dinner.

Sofia

MOUNTAIN VIEW

Sofia is next to Vitosha Mountain. The mountain is very beautiful and changes its colours every season.

MY HOME

Being together with friends and family is a big part of what we do – picnics or walks in the park or getting together for dinner. Bulgaria and the Balkans are known for having warm and emotional people who are very close to their families.

SUMMER FUN

We have four seasons, so the weather changes four times a year. Our favourite time is the summer when we get to go to the beach and spend a lot of time outside.

I like the snow in the winter.

My favourite thing is dancing.

Belgium

MATTHIAS
Age 9

My name is Matthias. I live in Kapellen, Belgium.

KAPELLEN

We live in Kapellen, Belgium, a quiet green area in a forest close to the city of Antwerp. We have a big garden and love to run around and play there. Close to our home is a nature reserve where we often go for long walks. In the spring, the whole area turns purple because there are lots of rhododendron flowers in the forest where we live.

MY THREE WORDS

STUBBORN **SMART** **MISCHIEVOUS**

MY FAMILY

I have two little twin brothers, and we always play together. And sometimes we fight. In summer we go to theme parks — we love rollercoasters, but most of all, we travel. I've been to many fantastic places with my parents, from Australia in the east to the USA in the west, from Italy in the south to Norway in the north.

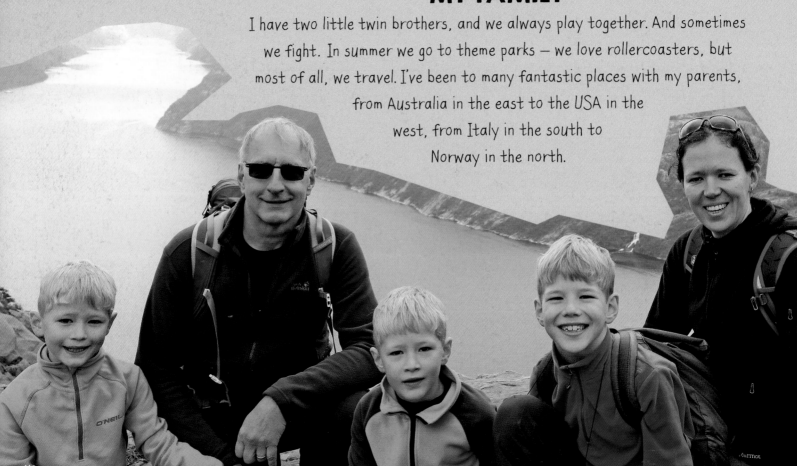

NO-GAMING ZONE

I play all kinds of board games, but chess, Monopoly™ and Cluedo™ are my favourites. My parents don't want me to play video games (we don't have any), so I only do it when I go to play at my friends' houses.

BELGIAN PRIDE

I LOVE Belgian chocolate, Belgian waffles and Belgian fries ... maybe that's the real reason I like living here so much!

MY FAVOURITE TOYS

I have many friends at school and one best friend. We play board games, Lego™ and chess together. I think he is my best friend because we share the same interests and we are always happy to see each other.

MY FAVOURITE ANIMAL

My favourite animal is a rabbit, but I don't have one as a pet. I do have a cat and some goldfish. The cat is not really mine. It arrived here about a year ago and never left. She seems to like us (and we like her!).

DREAM BIG

I love football, and I play on a team. Football is also the most popular sport in our country. My dream is to become a famous football player on a top team, or to become a millionaire. Sometimes I dream that I will invent a flying car.

MY HOBBIES

My other hobbies are drawing and playing music. I also love to read books, ride my bicycle and play with my brothers.

MATTHIAS

MAXIMUS
Age 9

My name is Maximus. I live in Kaunakakai, Molokai, Hawaii, USA.

MOLOKAI

Our island is known as 'The Friendly Isle'. There are only 7,000 people on Molokai. Where I live, I can see the ocean and two other islands.

MY FAMILY

In my family I have my mum, dad, two brothers and a cat. We like to go camping and to the beach together. My mum is a teacher, and my dad is a farmer.

GO FISH

In their spare time, the people in my community go to the beach, fish and hunt. I like to go diving and hunting with my dad.

MY THREE WORDS

NICE

FUN

COOL

Fast Fact: There are no traffic lights on Molokai. They're not needed. The island does not have much traffic.

HOT SPOT

It is hot where we live, and we don't get a lot of rain. It is always warm on our island.

TURN IT UP

I want to be a DJ when I grow up because I like music. I would like to visit Los Angeles in the USA because that's where the actors and singers are.

Fast Fact: Many people believe Molokai is where hula (a Hawaiian form of dance) began. A hula festival is held on the island each summer.

MY HOME

We live in a house. In our garden, we have chickens, goats and wild deer.

I like swimming. In my area, the most popular sport is baseball.

Colombia

MAYRA
AGE 9

My name is Mayra. I live in Santa Marta, Colombia.

SANTA MARTA
Santa Marta is a very pretty small city with many beautiful beaches and trees. It is very hot.

MY FAMILY
In my family, there's my mum, dad, my older sister and my little brother. My grandmother says I'm in the middle like cheese in a sandwich! My grandparents on my mother's side live in another village.

Santa Marta

MY FAVOURITE SUBJECT

I like art because I can be creative and feel free!

The sport that most people in my country like is football. I don't know why. To tell the truth, for me, it is very boring.

BUNNY LOVE

My favourite animal is a rabbit because it's an affectionate little fluffy thing. There are many rabbits at my grandparents' house.

BIG GOALS

My family work very hard in our shop. I don't want to do what my parents do. I want to do something more fun. I want to be a doctor and have a big house with cats and rabbits.

FUN ON WHEELS

My hobby is riding a bike! I meet my friends, who all have bikes, and we ride from corner to corner because my mum will not let me go any farther.

SUN AND SAND

My favourite places are the beaches here on the coast. There are so many and each one is different. Some are big and others are small.

My sister and me at the beach

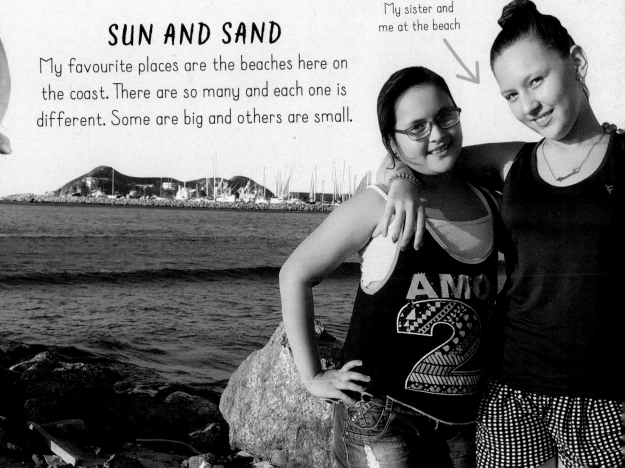

Ecuador

MELANI
AGE 8

My name is Melani. I live in Bua de los Colorados, Santo Domingo, Ecuador.

BUA DE LOS COLORADOS

This is a very tranquil place surrounded by nature. There are lots of birds that are always singing, which brings harmony to us. There are mountains and jungle, and the climate is tropical. It often rains a lot in the night.

MY THREE WORDS
Happy Happy Happy!

MY FAMILY

My family is one of the families that works to strengthen the Tsachila culture and to maintain our customs and roots. I like that my parents teach me and are examples of how to follow our customs and speak our native language – Tsafiki. I get on really well with my brothers and sisters. We all love each other.

My sisters and me

118

COOKING WITH FAMILY

I pretend to cook with my cousin and sister. I like to learn how to prepare our traditional foods. →

KEEPING TRADITIONS ALIVE

I like to do crafts and listen to the stories my father tells me that are part of our culture. He also teaches me to dance the marimba.

NO LITTERING!

I am afraid of the contamination of the river. I hate it when people come into our community and leave their rubbish here.

THREE LANGUAGES

I like to study English. It will be my third language. I try to do well in everything at school, but some subjects are harder than others.

FRUIT AND FOREST

I like the countryside, the forest and especially butterflies. I also like to collect fruit from all around at different times of the year.

A family home in the Tsachila community

MY HOUSE

My house is small with a big patio in front, and we have two traditional houses where we can receive visitors. There are chickens and piglets that eat anything they can find. We have a vegetable garden beside the house.

American Samoa

MICHAEL
Age 9

My name is Michael. I live on Tutuila Island in Aua, American Samoa.

Fast Fact: American Samoa is the only U.S. territory in the Southern Hemisphere.

TUTUILA ISLAND

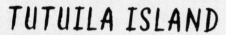

I live on a tropical island. We have really high mountains that are covered with lots and lots of green trees. Our oceans are blue and clear. It takes a day to travel from one end of the island to the other end. My village Aua — which is one of the biggest villages on the island — is located next to Pago Pago, the capital.

MY THREE WORDS
Kind, Obedient, Adventurous

MY FAMILY

In my house, there are only five of us: my papa (grandfather), mama (grandmother), my mum, my older brother and me. My mum does all the washing, cooking and cleaning and takes care of my mama and papa.

My mum and me

120

NO PLACE LIKE HOME

I haven't been anywhere else but here. I've never been on a plane or boat — not even to go to our neighbouring islands. But I would like to visit all the islands of Samoa and New Zealand one day.

FOOTBALL FANATIC

My favourite sport to play is American football. It gets me excited because at any moment, you can get hit by an opponent. But more importantly, you can hit back. Football is the biggest sport here in American Samoa.

SUNDAY FEAST

The second largest house on our land doesn't have walls because it is the *umu* (underground oven). This is where my family make the traditional Sunday *umu* for our Sunday *to'ona'i* (feast) after the morning church service.

Taro fruit

FAMILY HISTORY

My family have been here on the land that we live on for about 200 years. Our bathroom and shower are separated from the house. In front of our house are five graves, which are for our loved ones who have passed on.

WORK TOGETHER

My grandfather fixes cars and tends to his *ma'umaga* (plantation). The cars bring in some money while the plantation provides us with food like taro and banana. Everyone helps with the plantation since it's too big for my papa to run by himself.

United States

NATHEN
Age 11

My name is Nathen. I live in Baltimore, Maryland, USA.

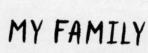

MY THREE WORDS
Intelligent
Athletic
Curious

BALTIMORE

I live in the city of Baltimore. It's not very quiet. There are lots of people who live near me. We have a neighbourhood playground, skyscrapers and lots of buildings.

MY FAMILY

I have a big family — two brothers and a sister! I live in Baltimore with my dad and stepmom, but my mom and little brother live in Virginia.

It's pretty cool to have two places I call home. I love to spend time with all my family, no matter where they live.

MY HOUSE

I live in a townhouse. We have three floors. I share a room with my brother, and my sister has her own room. We have a big kitchen, and I love cooking for my little sister.

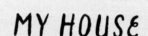

Baltimore

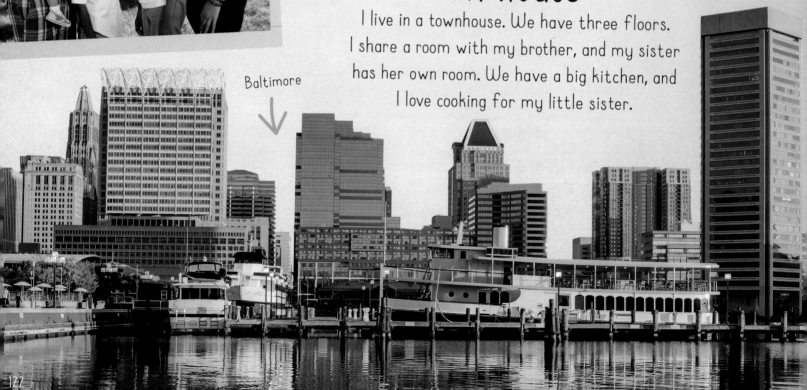

At school, I am in the robotics and chess clubs. I play video games on weekends.

LIVING HISTORY

My city has a lot of history behind it. Slowly but surely, my school and parents are teaching me some of it. For example, we live right down the street from Lexington Market. It's been in business since 1782 and has been standing ever since.

HOME TEAM

Baltimore is home to my favourite American football team — the Baltimore Ravens! I've been to a game before, and it was awesome. I was so close to the players, I could feel their hard work. We are also home to the Baltimore Orioles baseball team. It's so much fun to go to games in my own hometown.

My brother, my sister and me

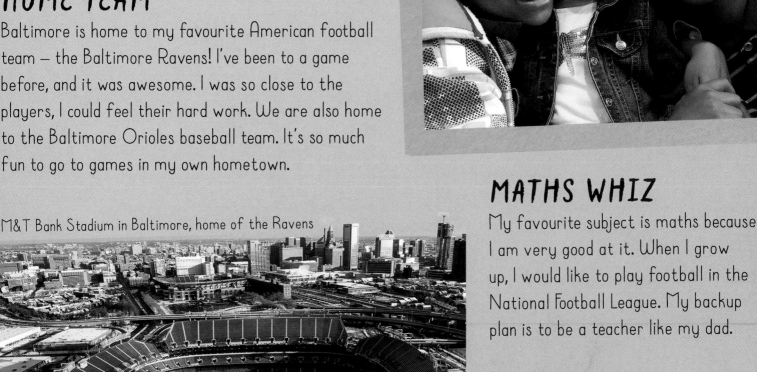

M&T Bank Stadium in Baltimore, home of the Ravens

MATHS WHIZ

My favourite subject is maths because I am very good at it. When I grow up, I would like to play football in the National Football League. My backup plan is to be a teacher like my dad.

NEVER QUIT

Playing in football games gets my heart pumping! A lot of my friends play football. I enjoy it. It's fun, and I like to see how much better I can be at it.

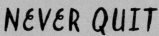

Fast Fact: Writer Edgar Allan Poe lived in Baltimore. The Baltimore Ravens were named after his poem 'The Raven'.

Kosovo

NEA
AGE 8

My name is Nea.
I live in Pristina, Kosovo.

MY THREE WORDS
Calm, Happy, Curious

PRISTINA

I live in a flat in Pristina. There is a lot of traffic from cars and buses and people going to work. It's a busy city. However, there is a huge park I go to with my mum, and we walk for hours.

MY FAMILY

My family is small. It is me and my mum, but I have many cousins. I love to help Mum in the kitchen, and we make spinach pie together. I love playing with the dough and rolling the pin.

SUMMER HOLIDAYS

My favourite place is Saranda, in southern Albania. It is special because my mum and I spend summers there. I love holidays because I get to spend more time with my cousins. It's time away from school and work, so we can have fun, swim and sightsee.
I enjoy the long drive in the car getting there.

Mum and me

Saranda, Albania

COUSIN TIME

My cousin Eran is my best friend. We go skiing and spend weekends and summers together. We also play football and Frisbee™ and giggle about the same things!

Eran and Me

MY FAVOURITE ANIMAL
Rabbit

Pristina, Kosovo

CREATIVE PLAY

My room is full of dolls — plastic, stuffed, singing — but I love making things out of clay, too. I also like Lego™ because I enjoy assembling the small pieces. Sometimes I get upset when I can't assemble them as fast as I want to.

SNOWY DAYS

Winters here are full of snow. Kids get to play with snow, make snowmen and have fun.

I love learning to play guitar.

Pristina, Kosovo

Egypt

NICOLE
AGE 9

My name is Nicole.
I live in Cairo, Egypt.

CAIRO

Cairo is a city that has many buildings and is always crowded. I live beside the Cairo International Airport, which is the main airport in Egypt. There are lots of people around me on the streets. I've become used to the noise they cause.

MY THREE WORDS
Caring, Creative, Active

MY FAMILY

My family includes my mum, dad, grandfather, grandmother and my pet dog, Jax. I don't have any brothers or sisters, but I have a cousin named Joe who is like a brother to me. We live in a flat on the first floor of a small building. My father's father built the building we live in.

Cairo

Kushari

MY FAVOURITE FOOD

My favourite Egyptian food is *kushari*. It's an Egyptian dish that is made of pasta — another favourite food of mine — lentils and rice.

BEACH DAY

My favourite thing to do on the weekend is to spend the day on the beach in Ain Sokhna on the Red Sea. Ain Sokhna is an hour and a half away from my home. I love running down the shore, playing in the sand and swimming with my cousin.

Ain Sokhna

MY SCHOOL

My school is unique because it's a small school for girls that teaches the American system. I have only nine girls in my class plus me. I get to school on the school bus. It is a bit far away, but when there is no traffic, I get there really fast.

SPRING CELEBRATIONS

My favourite holidays are Easter and Sham Elnessim (a day after Easter). Sham Elnessim is the day that Egyptians celebrate the beginning of spring. I love painting boiled eggs with my grandma and cousin.

SPORTS

I do gymnastics two times every week. The most popular sports in Egypt are football and handball.

Great Pyramids

LAND OF THE PHAROAHS

I love the history and culture that Egypt is so famous for. We are descendants of the famous pharaohs. The Great Pyramids of Giza are my favourite Egyptian monuments because the pharaohs built these big monuments to be buried in.

Japan

NOA
AGE 10

My name is Noa.
I live in Seiwadai-Higashi,
Kawanishi, Japan.

MY THREE WORDS

HARD-WORKING

CLUMSY

PERSISTENT

KAWANISHI

Kawanishi is known as an
old town – about 1,000
years old. It is surrounded
by mountains. We have
a river to catch fish and
lots of parks. There is
also a rare type of cherry
blossom tree, which is
really beautiful.

MY FAMILY

In my family, there is my father, mother, Shoma, Tenma
and me. My father is an electrician. Shoma and Tenma
are my brothers, who are twins. They are interested in
watching YouTube and playing games at the shopping
centre. We fight every day, but I love them!

MY HOUSE

I live in an old house – 40 years old. It has eight rooms, including four tatami mat rooms. I like this house because our living room is huge. There is a fireplace and *horigotatsu* (table-based heater) as well.

My bedroom

MY DINNER

I have been ← taking a Japanese calligraphy class for seven years.

TRADITION

I started taking a Japanese tea ceremony class two years ago.

MY FAVOURITE ANIMAL

Whales! Maybe I'll be a vet for whales when I grow up.

MY FAVOURITE PLACE

In Miyazu city in Kyoto, Japan, the ocean is very beautiful, and we can go fishing as well. We caught 34 fish in one go this summer!

United Arab Emirates

OWEN

My name is Owen.
I live in Dubai,
United Arab Emirates.

Age 10

DUBAI

People in Dubai are multicultural and come from all over the world. A lot of people come to visit Dubai, so it gets really busy, but not noisy at all.

MY FAMILY

My small family includes my dad, mum, sister and brother. My brother is only three years old, and my sister is five. We like to cook and gather round the table with family and friends.

MY THREE WORDS
Fun
Playful
Kind

LUXURY LIVING
Dubai is known for a luxury lifestyle, tall buildings and hot weather. People here like to go to the beach, the shopping centre and the park in their spare time.

SUNNY DAYS

We live in a hot country, with sunshine and wide beaches. I have never seen real snow.

TOP SPORTS

I love football, but swimming is my top favourite sport. It is common where I live. I also like dancing. I've joined my school production recently. I would like to be a PE teacher when I grow up. I love sports!

MY CITY

I live in the city in a quiet community where there are kids' parks and small shops.

FAVOURITE TRIP

Hong Kong Disneyland™ is my favourite place that I've visited. I enjoyed all the rides, and going there with my friends was extra fun. I also love Chinese food — especially noodles.

اوين

My name is Owen. It means 'help' in Arabic, and I like to help people.

Cambodia

PANHA
Age 11

My name is Panha.
I live in Steung Saen,
Cambodia.

STEUNG SAEN

I live in Steung Saen, Cambodia and
there are a lot of people here. Most of
the girls go to the riverside to exercise.
The boys here play a game where
they kick a plastic toy with feathers
back and forth.

MY FAMILY

My family is very big. My mum and
dad both work in an office. I have lots
of cousins, but no brothers or sisters.
My uncle teaches music and the Khmer
language. He likes to bring his students
to our house to play music for us. My
grandma always cooks for everyone.

MY THREE WORDS
Playful, Curious, Adventurous

WEATHER REPORT

The weather is tropical, so I have never seen snow.
We only have two seasons – rainy and dry. Where I live
is mostly flat. The people grow rice and vegetables.

Rice paddy

MY FAVOURITE SPORTS

I love swimming and cycling. I also like learning karate. In my province, a lot of people like to play football and volleyball.

CAT FAMILY

I have seven cats – three adults and four kittens. They don't all have names yet.

MY SCHOOL

I took a test to get into a special boarding school, and I passed the test. I live there now and am the second-youngest student in the school. My new nickname is 'Miss Snack' because when we went on an eight-day school trip, I was always eating snacks!

WHAT WILL I BE?

I don't know yet what I want to do when I grow up, but maybe I could be a doctor. I want to help the poor people in my country so that they can go to hospital for free.

Nigeria

PENIEL

Age 10

My name is Peniel. I live in Ilupeju, Lagos, Nigeria.

LAGOS

Lagos is a very big city. I live in a very loud environment with a lot of people around. There are many skyscrapers in Broad Street, a large business area on Lagos Island. I like the bright lights at night and the fun places to visit. It's very hot in the dry season and rains a lot during the rainy season.

MY FAMILY

I live with my aunt and uncle. I call them Mum and Dad. My aunt took me in when I was born, and she has always cared for me as a mother would. She is a banker and my uncle is an accountant. I also live with my grandma, my Aunt Folake (my uncle's younger cousin), my adopted sister, Peace, and my brothers (my aunt's sons). It's a large family of eight.

MY THREE WORDS
Hard-working, Caring, Helpful

Lagos

Lagos

MY HOME

I live in a two-bedroom flat. My mum and dad occupy one room. All the kids and Grandma occupy the second room. I like that we have a regular electricity supply.

LOVE FOR ALL

My family is a special one. Non-biological kids and biological kids are loved equally.

ON THE MOVE

I am athletic. I do a lot of running, football, skipping and jumping. I also like to dance.

MY FAVOURITE HOLIDAY

Christmas

ADD IT UP

My school is located very close to my house. I get there on foot. Maths is my favourite subject, and English is my least favourite. That's because I love to calculate more than sitting to read. I wish to become a banker or a doctor.

MY FAVOURITE FOOD

I love Indonesian noodles with eggs.

135

Liberia

RAJON
AGE 9

My name is Rajon.
I live in Monrovia, Liberia.

MONROVIA

Monrovia is a city with a lot of cars and people. Where I live is mostly quiet but can get very noisy sometimes — especially on the weekends.

MY THREE WORDS
Funny, Creative, Smart

MY FAMILY

My family includes my mum and dad, my older brother, Isaiah, and my younger sister, Sophia. I am very close to my siblings. We play together all of the time. Right now, we live in a flat, but my family is in the process of building a house.

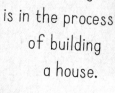

CHRISTMAS TOGETHER

My favourite holiday is Christmas. We usually spend it with my grandma on her farm.

MY HOME

I live on the top of a hill right next to the ocean. It is in the heart of the city.

GRANDMA'S FARM

My grandmother's farm is in Kingsville township about an hour away from my house. She grows rice, palm, plantains and cocoa. She also has a lot of animals like horses, pigs, cows and chickens. My favourite animal is a horse.

MY SCHOOL

My school is not like a regular school because we use computers a lot to do our work. I ride to school every morning with my brother and sister. Our driver takes us. My favourite subject is French because it is very fun trying to learn a new language.

RESTAURANT IN FRANCE

When I grow up, I would like to be a chef because I enjoy cooking. I would like to visit France because I am thinking of opening a restaurant there.

OUTDOOR SPORTS

During their spare time, the kids in my community play outside. My favourite sport is football, which is also very popular where I live.

Iceland

RAPHAËL
AGE 10

My name is Raphaël.
I live in Reykjavik, Iceland.

REYKJAVÍK

I like the weather in Iceland because it is never too warm. The sea is close by, and from there we see all the mountains on the other side of the bay. My street has a lot of houses, and the next street is my town's main street — with a lot of cafés, restaurants and shops selling tourist stuff.

MY THREE WORDS
Cool Karate Kid

MY FAMILY

My mum and dad both work in tourism. I feel a bit sorry for them because they type on the computer and talk on the phone all day, while I have a lot of fun at school and sports. I have an older brother, but he doesn't want to play a lot because he is six years older and has a girlfriend.

Reykjavik

OUT IN NATURE

I like hiking outdoors, especially when we go to a nature pool.

SNOW DAYS

I LOVE it when it snows, because then I can play in it — sledging, building snowmen and houses, and throwing snowballs. Summer is also good because it is light all night, and when I am in a cottage, I can play outside until late.

AT SCHOOL

My favourite subjects are arts and crafts and cooking because I get to take stuff home and give gifts.

My art

POWERFUL KICKS

I train in football with my local team, which is the most popular sport in my class. I also practise karate, and I just got an orange belt!

A BIT OF EVERYTHING

I am half French, half Icelandic, and I was born in England. I lived in Spain when I was little and I speak Icelandic, French and little bit of English and Spanish.

My favourite animal is Snorri, my hamster.

Ghana

SENAM
Age 9

My name is Senam.
I live in Amrahia, Ghana.

MY THREE WORDS

Friendly
Shy
Curious

AMRAHIA

We live in southern Ghana in the outskirts of a city called Accra, and it used to be very quiet. My parents built our house before I was born. Now Accra is coming closer, and we have more traffic jams. We can see the Akwapim Mountains from our house.

MY FAMILY

I have one sister who is six years old. My father is from Ghana, and my mother is from the Netherlands. When my parents met in 2003, they decided to live together in Ghana, and this is where I was born. My parents have a travel company and organise tourist trips to Ghana, Togo, Benin and Burkina Faso.

MY HOME

We have a cosy brick house and a veranda, and also an office and two guestrooms. Outside, I like to ride around on my bike.

AT SCHOOL

My favourite school subject is maths because it's not too difficult for me. I don't like language arts because I find it boring.

GAME NIGHT

I like to play a Ghanaian game called *Oware*, and board games with my mother.

Playing Oware with my sister

SISTER TIME

I share my room with my sister, and we like to play together, especially with our teddy bears. But we also fight, especially when we are allowed to play on the computer.

BEATING THE HEAT

It's hot in Ghana because we are just under the equator. They call it the tropics. I like swimming in the pool, which I do often, especially when it's hot.

MY FAVOURITE ANIMALS

I like snakes, dogs and cheetahs. We have snakes in Ghana, but no cheetahs.

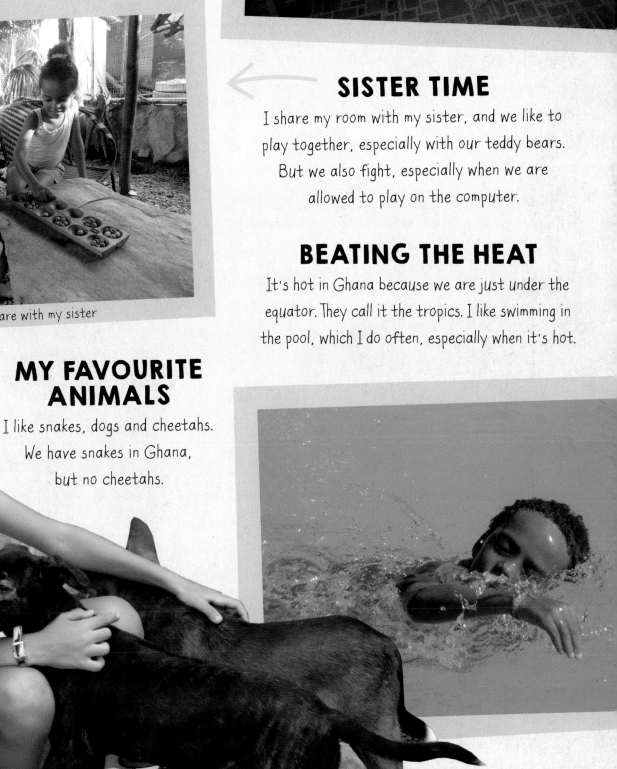

Paraguay

SHAWN
Age 8

My name is Shawn.
I live in Encarnación,
Paraguay.

MY THREE WORDS
Funny, Footballer, Explorer

ENCARNACIÓN
I live in Encarnación on the border of Argentina and Paraguay. It's a tourist city, and people come to visit the beach and the Jesuit ruins. It is very hot, and the soil is red.

MY FAMILY
My mum is a teacher, and my dad is a biologist and travel writer. My baby brother, Ewan, who is nine months old, likes to drink milk and steal my toys. I was so happy when my brother was born that I cried!

FOOTBALL FAN
I love football. I play for Club Universal and we are the city champions. My favourite teams are Real Madrid and Everton.

Encarnación

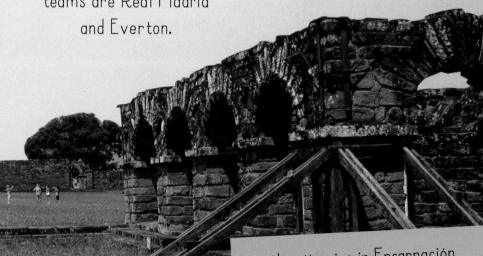
Jesuit ruins in Encarnación

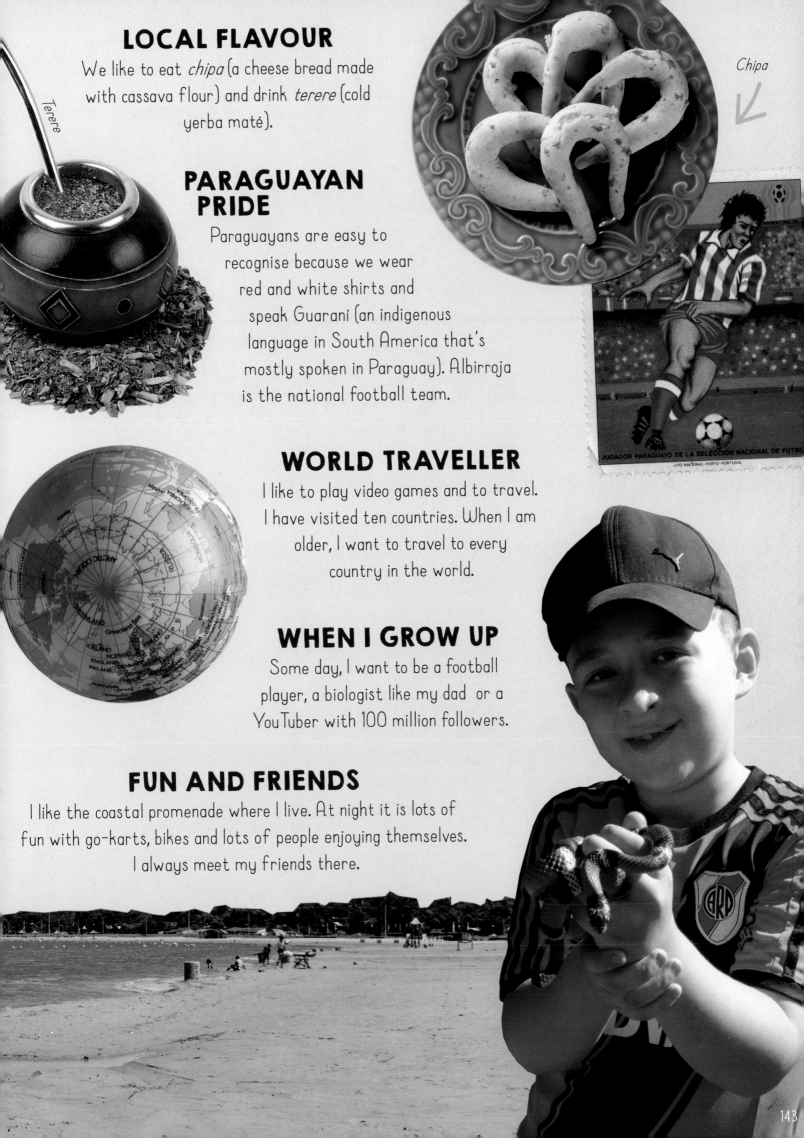

LOCAL FLAVOUR

We like to eat *chipa* (a cheese bread made with cassava flour) and drink *terere* (cold yerba maté).

Terere

Chipa

PARAGUAYAN PRIDE

Paraguayans are easy to recognise because we wear red and white shirts and speak Guarani (an indigenous language in South America that's mostly spoken in Paraguay). Albirroja is the national football team.

JUGADOR PARAGUAYO DE LA SELECCIÓN NACIONAL DE FUTBO

LITO NACIONAL - PORTO - PORTUGAL

WORLD TRAVELLER

I like to play video games and to travel. I have visited ten countries. When I am older, I want to travel to every country in the world.

WHEN I GROW UP

Some day, I want to be a football player, a biologist like my dad or a YouTuber with 100 million followers.

FUN AND FRIENDS

I like the coastal promenade where I live. At night it is lots of fun with go-karts, bikes and lots of people enjoying themselves. I always meet my friends there.

143

Jordan

SONDOUS AND TAMMEM AGE 8

Our names are
Sondous and
Tammem.
We are twins
who live in
Umm Sayhoun,
Petra, Jordan.

**SONDOUS:
MY THREE WORDS**
Pretty, Clever, Organised

**TAMMEM:
MY THREE WORDS**
Good, Funny, Interesting

UMM SAYHOUN

We live in a small village with one main street. Around our house, there are many sandstone mountains, but not many trees around. It is hot in the summer and very cold in the winter. It snows about once a year.

OUR FAMILY

In our family, there is our dad, Mahomoud, our mum, Fatima, our sister, Dalia, and us. Our dad is a tour guide, and our mum takes care of the family and the house. Sometimes our mum works, cooking food for tourists.

OUR HOME

We live in a flat upstairs from our grandmother. Our home is small, and we share a bedroom. In winter, we stay together in the living room to be close to the heater. In summer, we open all the windows and sometimes sit on the balcony at night.

SPORTS

Football is the most popular sport in our area. Other than that, there are not many sports in our village.

BEDOUIN PEOPLE

Where we live, there are Bedouin (nomadic Arab people), usually wearing a *thobe* – a one-piece dress. Men wear headscarves with black rings. Older women wear black dresses mostly – with black headscarves.

FAVOURITE SUBJECTS

I like Arabic lessons because they've improved my reading skills.

GO FLY A KITE

Many children here play with kites. They also like to play in the street with their friends, and after school they also help their mums with shopping.

In school, I like computer classes.

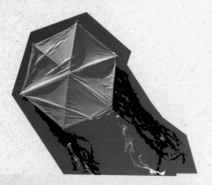

Petra

ANCIENT WONDER

We live near a very famous place called Petra, and we like to walk and hike there. It is one of the new Seven Wonders of the World. It's a huge place with carved caves, and it's 2,000 years old. Our mum was born there. Most of the time, we climb to a place called the Monastery.

Slovenia

STELA
Age 8

My name is Stela.
I live in Ljubljana, Slovenia.

LJUBLJANA

I live in a small block of flats near the city centre. From my kitchen window, I can see snow-capped mountains in the distance. The neighbourhood is filled with small buildings and lots of parks with small playgrounds. There are no skyscrapers around us.

COFFEE BREAK

On weekends, people here love to go into the city centre, buy food at the market and have coffee on the banks of Ljubljanica River.

MY THREE WORDS
Tall, Artistic, Curious

MY FAMILY

My family is my mum, my dad and my sister, Tesa. Tesa is five years old. As a family, we love to bake — apple pie is our favourite. We spend our free time exploring Slovenia or travelling abroad.

My family and me, when my sister and I were little

CITY OF BRIDGES

Ljubljana has lots of bridges. There's one with dragons because the dragon is the symbol of the city.

EXPLORE THE OUTDOORS

We all like to hike, and there are plenty of options in and around Ljubljana.

FROSTY FUN

We have snow in the winter. That's when we use the small hills in the neighbourhood to ride on our sledges. It gets so cold that the pond near our home freezes, and we can ice skate there.

IN A FOG

Ljubljana is so famous for its fog, it's often called 'White Ljubljana'.

CLIMB AND SLIDE

I love to play in playgrounds.

Denmark

SVEND
AGE 10

My name is Svend.
I live in Egebjerg,
Denmark.

MY THREE WORDS

FAIR
SMART
NICE

EGEBJERG

We live in a small village called
Egebjerg, a short distance from
the local town centre of Horsens.
Denmark has a very long coastline,
and I live close to the sea. The
weather is not extreme. We
normally don't have hurricanes,
snowstorms or huge floods.

MY FAMILY

There are five people in my family. I have
a little brother named Aksel (six years)
and a little sister named Agnes (two
years). My mum works as a high school
teacher, and my father works in a bank.
All the boys in my family like football,
and we play in the garden and watch
matches on TV.

BAND TOGETHER

Once a week I play keyboard in a band. I was taught piano for three years, but now I think it's more fun to play with other kids than by myself.

MY HOME

We live in a villa. All the kids have their own room. The kitchen and living room is one big room, and we spend most of our time there. We have a nice view over the fields and a big garden.

MANY MATCHES

I play football two times a week, and I often have matches on the weekends as well.

MY SCHOOL BAG

AT SCHOOL

My favourite subjects are PE and swimming. My least favourite subject is Danish, because it's very hard to learn.

MY BREAKFAST

SKY MOUNTAIN

There are no mountains in Denmark but there is a hill called 'Sky Mountain' which is only around 150 m (492 feet).

149

Australia

TEMPERANCE
Age 7

My name is Temperance.
I live in Lolworth Station,
Queensland, Australia.

LOLWORTH

Lolworth is dusty and has lots of trees. It is hot most of
the time, but when we get rain, it rains hard. There are
not many people around. Our neighbours live far away.
Everyone who lives with us works for Dad. It is beautiful
here, and we have mountains on the outskirts of our land.

MY FAMILY

In my family it's Mum, Dad, me, Peyton,
Florence and Duke. I have two sisters and one
brother. We live in a four-bedroom bungalow.

MY THREE WORDS
Nice, Sweet, Loving

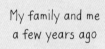
My family and me
a few years ago

HAPPY TOGETHER

I love that my family is small, and we go
motorbike riding and horse riding.

HOMESCHOOLER

I get homeschooled, and my teacher lives with us. In the garden, there is a classroom. Sometimes we have to go camping somewhere on the land to do the mustering (rounding up cattle) and have to do schoolwork in the camp in the dust.

FREE TIME

I like to read and dance around the house. I also like to do cartwheels and gymnastics things at home.

SPRING CHASE

The spring is the best part of the year. We can build dams, but my favourite bit is branding because we can chase the cattle and make them go into the race (loading chute).

LONG LIST

We have to travel two hours to go food shopping, so we have to buy lots at one time.

OUR CATTLE

We sell cows to the meat works so we can live and have money. I like doing cattle work. I sometimes go in our helicopter to check the water to make sure our cattle have enough to drink.

Vietnam

THAO MY
Age 9

My name is Thao My. I live in Mai Chau, Vietnam.

MAI CHAU

Our village is in Mai Chau valley – the mountainous area in northern Vietnam. It has beautiful scenery, and many people come to visit. It is normally quiet and peaceful, but gets very busy during weekends.

MY FAMILY

There are five people in my family: my grandmother, my father, my mother, my little sister, Linh and me. My little sister is just three months old. My grandmother was a farmer. She now stays at home doing housework. My father works for a tour company, and my mother works as a teacher at the local nursery school.

MY THREE WORDS
Active, Friendly, Confident

MY HOUSE

Everyone in my village and I are part of the Thai ethnic minority. We live in houses on stilts. In my home, we have a large living room, and the kitchen and toilet are separate from the house. Sometimes we welcome visitors to come and stay.

Mai Chau

AFTER SCHOOL

I like hanging around my house after school. We have a big space where I can play with my friends. In my free time, I love reading books and watching kids' programmes on TV.

A POPULAR SPORT

My favourite sport is badminton although I am not very good at it. That is also a popular sport in my village.

MY DREAM TRIP

I dream to visit Ho Chi Minh City, Vietnam. I have never been there, but I heard it is very different from my village. There is also a lot of good food there I want to try. I love food.

FOUR SEASONS

There are four seasons in Mai Chau: rainy and humid in the spring, very hot in the summer, cool in the autumn, and very cold in the winter. I love summer the most because we have a long summer break, and I go travelling with my family.

WHEN I GROW UP

I love drawing, so my favourite school subject is art. I want to be a teacher like my mum. I love kids, and I like teaching them.

Mai Chau

Fast Fact: There are 54 ethnic groups in Vietnam. About 1.5 million people are part of the Thai ethnic minority, less than 2% of Vietnam's population.

Argentina

TOBIAS
Age 9

My name is Tobias.
I live in Buenos Aires,
Argentina.

BUENOS AIRES

We live in a very big city called Buenos Aires near a river called Rio de la Plata. It is nice and has pretty parks. My favourite park is Palermo. There are lots of bikes and people running. There is also a lake there, and sometimes we rent a boat.

MY THREE WORDS
Fun, Good Friend

Palermo park

MY FAMILY

There are four people in my family — my mother, my father, my brother, Camilo, and me. Camilo is four years old. We live in a house in a quiet area. It has a garden where I can play football and invite friends over.

GOOD NIGHTS

One of my favourite things is *pijamadas*. That is inviting friends to sleep at my house and playing with them until very late at night. I also like sleeping very much. I hate when my brother wakes me up early!

Buenos Aires

AT SCHOOL

My favourite subject is natural science, mainly because I love animals. My least favourite is grammar. I hate to write a lot.

NATIONAL PASTIME

I like playing football very much. Everybody in Argentina loves football! I also like watching movies on my tablet computer and playing on my PlayStation 4®.

SOUTHERN SNOW

In the south of Argentina, in a town called Ushuaia, it snows a lot. I enjoy going there and playing in the snow.

MY FAVOURITE TREAT

I love *dulce de leche* (heated sweetened condensed milk).

HAPPY CAMPERS

As a family, we enjoy travelling together and spending time in nature. Once we went to an island in Baja California called Espiritu Santo. We camped there and it was the best. No electricity, no toilet, but a lot of fun.

Mexico

VALENTINA
AGE 7

My name is Valentina.
I live in Puerto Escondido
in Oaxaca, Mexico.

MY THREE WORDS
Happy, Beautiful, Fun

MY HOUSE

I live in a new house. We've been here for maybe one month.
It has two storeys. We eat in the kitchen on the first floor.
There is also a room that we rent to people. I like this house
because it is nearer to the ocean than our last one. I like it
also because it has a big garden to play in.

MY FAMILY

In Puerto Escondido, I have my mother, my brother, Dammian – who is 14 – and
Ziggy, my stepfather. My mother gives Spanish lessons to adults. My stepfather works
as a scuba-diving instructor. I have grandparents, cousins, great-grandparents, and
many more people in my family in Chile. *Muchas más!*

SURF'S UP

I like surfing. I can
sometimes surf all by
myself. My brother taught
me. I am not afraid.

EXPLORING THE MARKET

In my village, there are always people around. In town, there is a market where we can buy toys, oranges, limes, bananas and lettuce. It's fun to go and see everything in the market and buy things.

Enchiladas salsa verde

MY FAVOURITE FOODS

Sometimes we go to restaurants in town, and I eat hotcakes with melon, and banana with honey. I also eat enchiladas salsa verde without cheese.

LOCAL FAIRS

I like going to fairs because there are games and rides. In November, there are fairs in my town for the Day of the Dead.

MAKING WAVES

I love the ocean because it's fun to dive into the waves, swim and see fish. I can also play with my friends and make sandcastles. There are crabs on the beach!

Russia

VICTOR
Age 7

My name is Victor. I live in St. Petersburg, Russia.

MY THREE WORDS
Strong, Nimble, Smart

ST. PETERSBURG
St. Petersburg has many rivers, canals and bridges — and a lot of museums. It's considered to be the cultural capital of Russia. I like the aqua park most of all.

MY FAMILY
First we had three people in our family — mum and dad and me. Now it's us plus Murzik the kitten! Oh, and grandma. But she doesn't live with us. She lives nearby, and we go to visit. She picks me up from school sometimes. I also have a big sister, but she lives in Moscow.

St. Petersburg

MY HOME

I live in a flat in a big square building with a courtyard in the middle. It has nine floors. I have my own room, with maps on the walls, a bed, a sports corner and a mini wardrobe. There's a table and a lot of school notebooks. And Murzik — most importantly!

SUN, WHERE ARE YOU?

In St. Petersburg, it's almost always cloudy, foggy and sad. No sun at all! Haven't had a single ray of sunshine in ages. In the summer, we have sun sometimes, but at that time I usually leave the city. Winters are wet and snowy, so the sun never shows up.

My favourite animal MURZIK!

LEGO™ ALL DAY

Most of all I love building Lego™! I can do it all day. Sometimes I get up to stretch because my back gets really stiff.

POWERFUL MOVE

I do karate, and I also like football and cycling. Once Mum wanted to brush my hair. I decided to show her what they just taught us at karate and knocked the brush out of her hand (but carefully). And then I did it again. The third time I did it I broke it in half — a thick plastic brush!

HOT ICE, COOL SCIENCE

What would I like to do when I grow up? Something connected with science! I love all kinds of experiments. Once I mixed Dad's deodorant, toothpaste, some creams and powders, and when I froze it, it turned into hot ice! Hot ice, can you imagine?!

159

Ethiopia

YARED
Age 7

My name is Yared. I live in Mekele, Ethiopia.

MY THREE WORDS

Happy
Handsome
Smart

MELEKE

Mekele is a big city. There are lots of tall buildings. Near my house, you can see horses and carts, donkeys, cars and *Bajaj* (scooters).

MY FAMILY

I live in one room with my mother, whose name is Hiwot. I call her Hiwot and sometimes Mama. The other rooms have another family, and they have a maid. We have a toilet, which we share with the other people. We wash in our room with water in a bowl.

My street

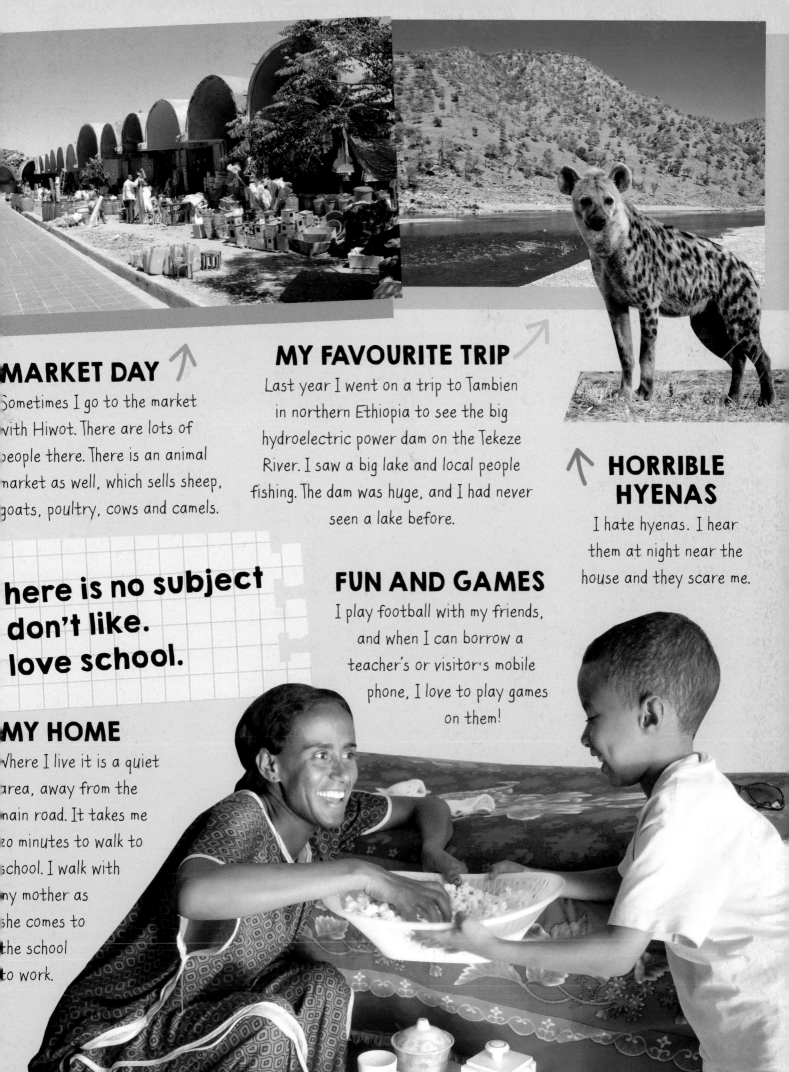

MARKET DAY ↑

Sometimes I go to the market with Hiwot. There are lots of people there. There is an animal market as well, which sells sheep, goats, poultry, cows and camels.

MY FAVOURITE TRIP ↗

Last year I went on a trip to Tambien in northern Ethiopia to see the big hydroelectric power dam on the Tekeze River. I saw a big lake and local people fishing. The dam was huge, and I had never seen a lake before.

↑ ## HORRIBLE HYENAS

I hate hyenas. I hear them at night near the house and they scare me.

There is no subject I don't like. I love school.

FUN AND GAMES

I play football with my friends, and when I can borrow a teacher's or visitor's mobile phone, I love to play games on them!

MY HOME

Where I live it is a quiet area, away from the main road. It takes me 20 minutes to walk to school. I walk with my mother as she comes to the school to work.

161

South Korea

YEONWOO
AGE 9

My name is Yeonwoo.
I live in Seoul,
South Korea.

SEOUL

In Seoul, there are mountains and the Han River.
The Han River is like a sea. People love to go there
in the summer to avoid the heat, but swimming is
not allowed. We also have Hongjecheon, a stream
with good places for cycling and walking.

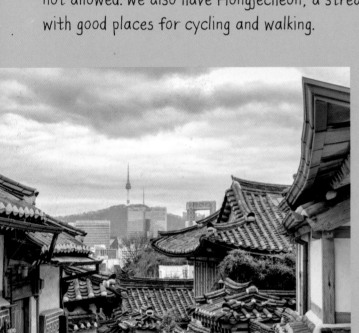

Seoul

MY THREE WORDS
Fun, Smart, Confident

MY FAMILY

I live with my mum, dad and little sister, who is four
years old. My mum is a pharmacist. She always helps
me with my homework and explains things easily. My
dad works at a publishing
company. He is kind and
fun. My little sister, Yeonsoo,
goes to nursery school, and
she listens to most of my
requests, which makes me feel
like a queen.

MY BEDROOM

I live in a block of flats in Seoul, and it is quite big — 4,300 flats are there! My room is like a princess' room. I designed my bed, and a carpenter made it.

A LITTLE CORNY

Yeonsoo and I like corn, so we go to Moraenae market — the traditional market — to buy it. Actually, we are very lucky because it is quite hard to buy corn in Seoul.

FEATHERED FRIEND

When we moved into our flat two years ago, my mum promised we could get a bird, so we recently got a yellow parrot named Norangi. It was scary when he flew at first, but we are becoming familiar with it.

MY SCHOOL

My school is a Christian mission school. I mostly like Korean and Bible studies. My least favourite school subject is maths. It is sometimes difficult. I really like school and my friends and teachers.

MY BREAKFAST

I have Korean food and American-style food as well. I love Mummy's spaghetti and Dad's ramen (noodles).

CREATIVE KID

I like drawing, reading books and playing *gayageum* — a Korean zither with 12 strings. I won two prizes in an art contest, and I am very proud of it.

My drawing

China

YITONG
AGE 7

My name is Yitong.
I live in Shanghai, China.

MY THREE WORDS
Good, Naughty, Friendly

SHANGHAI

Shanghai is a modern city with skyscrapers everywhere, but nearby there is countryside with beautiful waterside villages. There are two busy airports and lots of name brand shops.

MY FAMILY

I have a small family. My father is a finance manager and likes playing footall. My mother is a purchasing manager, and she loves movies and travelling. I am the only child. I like my parents so much!

MY FAVOURITE ANIMAL
Birds

Fast Fact: In China, noodles are a traditional birthday food, symbolising a long life. Often the noodles are one long, unbroken strand.

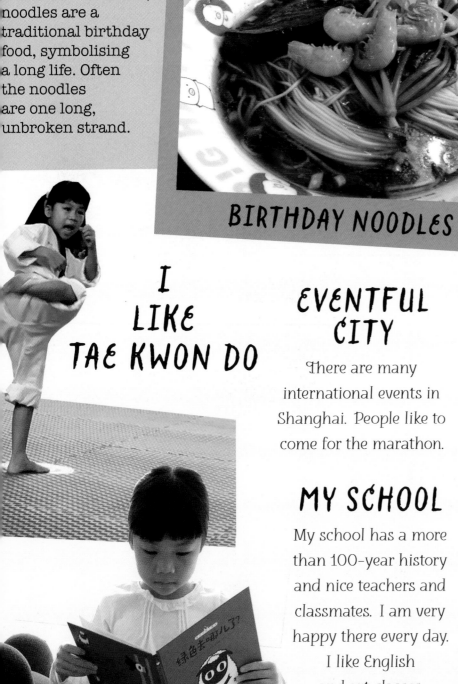

BIRTHDAY NOODLES

I LIKE TAE KWON DO

EVENTFUL CITY

There are many international events in Shanghai. People like to come for the marathon.

MY SCHOOL

My school has a more than 100-year history and nice teachers and classmates. I am very happy there every day. I like English and art classes.

DESIGNER DREAMS

I like drawing. I want to be a fashion designer like Coco Chanel and have my own studio. I can work in the back and open a shop in the front.

MY HOME

We live in a flat with two bedrooms.

Jordan

YOUSEF
AGE 10

My name is Yousef. I am from Syria, and I live in a refugee camp in Jordan.

THE REFUGEE CAMP

I live in a refugee camp in the middle of the desert. A lot of Syrian refugees are in this camp. You can see all the caravans (shelters) and lots of bikes, but not many trees. It is a desert, so the days are hot in summer. The nights are always cold. It rains a lot in winter also.

MY FAMILY

We are a big family. We are nine in the house, and I am the youngest. At the moment, we are on school holiday, so I spend more time with my family in our caravan — playing, eating and dancing.

MY HOME

My home now is three caravans next to each other, bordered with metal. Five of us sleep in one caravan, and the rest are in the other caravans with my father and my mother.

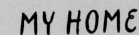

MINT GARDEN

We have planted some mint outside our caravan, and we have it with tea.

I want to be a famous singer.

WAR CHILD CENTRE

I like volleyball and football. I go to the War Child UK centre to play.

CAMP LIFE

People here spend their day in the streets, chatting with each other. Some people have work. The camp is known for the wedding parties in the evenings.

LET'S DANCE

I like dancing the *Dabka*, a traditional dance.

PLACE TO PLAY

In Syria, I liked to go to theme parks. Now we have a small place to play games in the camp.

Germany

YUKI
Age 9

My name is Yuki.
I live in Isernhagen, Germany.

ISERNHAGEN

I live in a village on the outskirts of the city of Hannover in a northern part of Germany. Isernhagen is a rural village, but close to the city of Hannover, so a lot of people work in the city and live in the countryside.

MY THREE WORDS
Sporty, Happy, Self-confident

MY FAMILY

My mother is an architect, and my father is a manager in the automobile industry. I have a brother, Niko, who is a few years older than me. Although I do like to have him around, we tend to fight about little things. (Too often if you ask my mum.)

PLAYFUL PET

We have a dog named Ebi — after my favourite sushi. She is almost two years old and still has a lot to learn. Apart from normal dog things, she loves to play with old towels, tear cardboard boxes into little pieces and sometimes even chew my socks.

MY HOUSE

The village of Isernhagen is lined with traditional German-style houses. Some of them are quite old, but most are fairly new. I live in a house with a garden.

HAPPY NAME

I was born in Tokyo, Japan, but we moved away when I was little. Yuki is a Japanese name and means 'happiness'.

HORSE COUNTRY

This area is well-known for its horses and even has its own breed called Hannoverian.

ALWAYS ACTIVE

I like to be active and have a lot of hobbies. My favourite sports at the moment are swimming and badminton. Last summer I finished my second triathlon.

NO HILLS HERE

This part of Germany is very flat. Actually, there are no hills at all. Lots of fields and patches of forest.

169

Morocco

ZAYAN
AGE 8

My name is Zayan, and
I live near Agadir, Morocco.

ZAYAN

We don't have a lot of rain, and I have only seen two or three storms in my life. It is around 15°C (59°F) in the winter and 25°C (77°F) in the summer. Once or twice a year for two or three days, there is the *chergui* – the wind from the Sahara. It gets very, very hot, but my house stays cool because there are thick walls.

MY THREE WORDS
Cute, Nice, Small

MY FAMILY

In my family, there is my dad, my mother, my big brothers, Adam and Ayman, and me. My father runs an eco lodge, and my mother is a teacher. Adam plays video games and chats with his friends, and Ayman is usually in the garden taking care of the animals or building a hut.

MY HOME

The eco lodge where we live is like a castle. It is orange because it is made with earth and little pieces of straw. There is a garden with animals like a farm. There are peacocks, chickens, goats and sheep. In my bedroom, there are blue bunk beds, and I sleep on the upper one.

Fast Fact:
An eco lodge is a place for tourists to stay that is built and run in a way that is kind to the surrounding environment.

STRIKE A POSE

I like yoga. I do it at school and at home with my mother.

Tajine

ARGAN FOREST

Where I live, it's very quiet. It is an argan forest. Here the forest doesn't have a lot of trees. There are goats and shepherds and Berber villages. We can walk in the hills, and we can see the city of Agadir and the ocean.

Fast Fact: Berbers are the indigenous peoples of Northwest Africa.

LET'S EAT

At home, we eat many different kinds of *tajines* (stews), couscous, fish, lentils, chicken, fruits and goat cheese. My favourite food is the couscous my aunt makes. We drink green tea made with mint, lavender and sage. But me, I prefer mint tea.

SECRET LANGUAGE

I speak Berber with my family and French with my mother. At school, I speak French and Arabic. It's nice because sometimes my brothers and I can tell secrets in Berber and my mother doesn't understand.

HORSING AROUND

My favourite sport is horse riding. I practise it twice a week. I can also ride a donkey. To make a donkey move, we say, 'Irra'. To make it stop, we say, 'Hush'.

QUIZ

How much did you discover about the kids of *This Is My World*? Take this quiz to find out! If you don't know the answer, flip back through the pages to search for clues.

1. Whose name means 'rain'?

2. Who doesn't have school on Wednesdays?

3. Who must travel by plane or boat to get to the next town?

4. Who lost two teeth in one day?

5. Who enjoys ice fishing and is part of two whaling crews?

6. Who loves his country's famous waffles and fries?

7. Who lives on 'The Friendly Isle'?

8. Whose name means 'help' in Arabic?

9. Who plays a game called Oware?

10. Who lives in a place where olives grow?

11. Who lives in a place that is 2,000 years old and famous for its carved caves?

12. Who loves trains more than anything else?

13. Who enjoys stilt walking?

14. Whose environmentally friendly community does not allow private cars?

15. Who lives in a city that is famous for its fog. . . and its dragons?

16. Who lives near a butterfly farm?

17. Who has to travel two hours to go food shopping?

18. Whose brother taught her how to surf?

19. Who loves whales?

20. Who lives near a famous waterfall?

21. Who plays Gaelic football?

22. Who lives in a valley near the Himalayas?

23. Who lives in a house on stilts?

24. Who has an orange-green belt in Krav Maga?

25. Who accidentally swam with a caiman?

26. Who has a hamster named Snorri?

27. Who plays percussion in a school band?

INDEX

PICTURE CREDITS